ROUTLEDGE LIBRARY EDITIONS:
ETHICS

Volume 36

MORAL JUDGEMENT

MORAL JUDGEMENT

DAVID DAICHES (D. D.) RAPHAEL

Routledge
Taylor & Francis Group
LONDON AND NEW YORK

First published in 1955 by George Allen & Unwin Ltd

This edition first published in 2021
by Routledge
2 Park Square, Milton Park, Abingdon, Oxon OX14 4RN

and by Routledge
52 Vanderbilt Avenue, New York, NY 10017

Routledge is an imprint of the Taylor & Francis Group, an informa business

British Library Cataloguing in Publication Data
A catalogue record for this book is available from the British Library

ISBN: 978-0-367-85624-3 (Set)
ISBN: 978-1-00-305260-9 (Set) (ebk)
ISBN: 978-0-367-50886-9 (Volume 36) (hbk)
ISBN: 978-1-00-305167-1 (Volume 36) (ebk)

Publisher's Note
The publisher has gone to great lengths to ensure the quality of this reprint but points out that some imperfections in the original copies may be apparent.

Disclaimer
The publisher has made every effort to trace copyright holders and would welcome correspondence from those they have been unable to trace.

MORAL JUDGEMENT

BY

D. DAICHES RAPHAEL

LONDON

GEORGE ALLEN & UNWIN LTD

RUSKIN HOUSE MUSEUM STREET

FIRST PUBLISHED IN 1955

PRINTED IN GREAT BRITAIN
in 11 point Baskerville
BY WILLMER BROTHERS AND CO. LTD
BIRKENHEAD

ACKNOWLEDGEMENTS

Dr. E. F. Carritt and Professor W. G. Maclagan have read the typescript of this book and have enabled me, by their criticism, to remove a number of blemishes. It goes without saying that neither of them would be prepared to subscribe to the views which I put forward. Indeed they strongly dissent from some of my main suggestions. I am therefore all the more grateful to them for the care with which they have scrutinized defects in the presentation of my position. I have also received helpful advice and criticism from Messrs. Allen & Unwin's reader.

Most of Chapter V has previously been printed, as an article entitled 'Justice and Liberty', in the *Proceedings of the Aristotelian Society*, New Series, Vol. LI (1950–51), and most of Chapter X, as an article entitled 'Causation and Free Will', in *The Philosophical Quarterly*, Vol. 2, No. 6 (January, 1952). I am indebted to the Editors and Publishers of those two journals for permission to reproduce this material.

I wish to express my warm thanks to the Carnegie Trust for the Universities of Scotland, which has provided a guarantee against loss in the publication of the book.

D.D.R.

Glasgow
1954

CONTENTS

I
INTRODUCTION

This book is concerned with two problems of moral philosophy. The first of these has often been treated as the problem of finding a common criterion for all right action; or again, as the relation between the right and the good. Considered a little more generally, it is the attempt to systematize or render coherent the content of moral judgements. In referring to earlier theories, I have dealt with this first problem largely as the battle-ground between utilitarianism and deontology. As between those two theories, I side with deontology; but I accept the criticism that it is unsatisfactory to leave principles of obligation in 'an unconnected heap', and I try to unify them by means of the Kantian principle of treating persons as ends-in-themselves. The attempt to do so requires an interpretation of that principle, and in my interpretation I reach a view of moral obligation which owes much to Hume and Adam Smith, and something to Martin Buber.

The second problem is the nature of moral judgement. This is the battle-ground between naturalism and non-naturalism or ethical intuitionism. I use the term 'naturalism' to include any theory which explains the meaning and function of ethical words wholly by reference to human nature, and which denies that the facts to be taken into account include entities or characteristics transcending human thoughts, conations, and feelings. I call naturalistic not only a theory which says that ethical words *describe* human attitudes, but also a theory which says that the function of such words is to *express* or *evoke* human attitudes. Mr. R. M. Hare, in his recent book, *The Language of Morals*,[1] confines the name to the first of these two kinds of theory, on the ground that only the first kind commits what Professor Moore called the naturalistic fallacy. Although the expression 'naturalistic fallacy' was introduced by Professor Moore in *Principia*

[1]Especiall y p. 82.

Ethica, the term 'naturalism' is much older. It seems to me that the issue between naturalism and intuitionism is ultimately a metaphysical one (though the name 'intuitionism' suggests a purely psychological or epistemological theory), namely whether there are entities or characteristics of goodness and rightness transcending the feelings, conations, and thoughts, of men. It is not merely a linguistic issue about the kind of function performed by normative words.

On this conflict between naturalism and intuitionism I reach no clear-cut solution. Intuitionists usually hold that moral judgements on individual actions or on particular classes of action express independent intuitions of transcendent truth. I argue that this theory is not necessary, and that a satisfactory hypothesis can be provided by a form of naturalism (in the wide sense of that term). But this hypothesis includes the view that principles of obligation fall under a single ultimate principle, and the old problem reappears at a new level when I ask whether the ultimate principle may be treated simply as a postulate or must be considered an axiom intuited as self-evident. At this level, I find myself unable to take a decisive view one way or the other.

Deontology has usually gone hand in hand with intuitionism. Since I reject the common type of intuitionism, and at least leave the door open for the dismissal of intuition even at the final stage, my view might be called 'deontology without intuitionism'. Again, my theory of moral obligation might be described as 'Kant in naturalistic dress'. Both these titles seem odd in the light of the history of moral philosophy. One of the purposes of my book is to separate the epistemological and metaphysical theories of deontologists from their examination of the relations between moral concepts. The latter is their strong suit. Their intuitionism has been much assailed in recent years, and as a result the properly ethical side of their theory has been neglected as if it did not greatly matter, and almost as if it had to stand or fall with the intuitionism. I think Professor Ayer wrote somewhere that the adoption of a naturalistic view of moral judgement has no effect on disputes about the criterion of right action. But in practice, modern naturalists tend to confine themselves to the former problem, and either show no interest in the latter or else assume—no doubt because of the historical connexion between naturalism and utilitarianism—that the correct view of the criterion of right action is a utilitarian one.

The two problems with which I am concerned cannot be altogether divorced from each other. When I try to unify the various principles of obligation under Kant's principle of ends, I must say how I interpret Kant's principle and how I think all instances of the concept of moral obligation exemplify it; and this involves giving an account of the nature of moral obligation and of the judgements which employ the concept. But I think that the relation between the two problems has been a little confused by discussion, in recent decades, of the 'definition' or 'meaning' of ethical terms. The definition of one ethical term by reference to others is part of my first problem, the systematization of the content of moral judgements. Explanation of the 'meaning' or function of ethical terms by reference to the psychological circumstances of their employment belongs to my second problem.

In order to mark the distinction between the two problems at the level at which they can be kept separate, I have called the first an investigation of the *logic of morals*. The expression 'the logic of' has been so loosely bandied about in recent philosophical discussion that I am a little reluctant to use it, especially since the fashionable employment of it seems to include, and at times to be confined to, the kind of examination of 'meaning' that I have assigned to my second problem. Linguistic philosophers sometimes tell us that their so-called 'logical' inquiry into language is a study of the way in which sentences and words 'behave' or of the 'jobs' that words perform. This is a kind of behavioural linguistics. It is both narrower and wider than what I have in mind; narrower, because it cuts out the consideration of intentional meaning; wider, because (to use the technical terminology of Charles W. Morris's 'Semiotic') it includes 'semantics' and 'pragmatics' as well as 'syntactics', while I wish to confine logic to 'syntactics'. I mean the clarifying of the relations of implication which hold between a group of concepts and judgements, and consequently the clarifying of such system or coherence as the group possesses. This task is analogous to that of formal logic in being concerned with relations of implication. Unlike formal logic, however, it takes account of the content of concepts and judgements, and not merely of empty forms. It is an *application* of formal logic to a specific field of thought (or, if you will, a specific field of discourse). Such an attempt to clarify the logical relations of concepts and to systematize them is a necessary part of the application of philosophy to any field of thought (or 'language'). The philosophy of science, or of particular sciences, includes a consideration of the logic of scientific concepts in my sense of the word 'logic'. Similarly, we have the philosophy, including the logic, of morals, art, religion, history, and politics. Ethics or moral philosophy is the application of philosophical tools to moral judgement and experience. The philosophical examination of moral judgement includes an examination of what I call the logic of morals.

I have called the second part of my book the *metaphysic of morals*. Here I must plead guilty to using the word 'metaphysic' very loosely. The term 'metaphysics' is a philosophical rag-bag. It has been used for ontology, for a synthesis of all knowledge and experience, for an examination of presuppositions, for speculative analogies from the particular to the highly general, and no doubt for other things as well. I have done little to sort the rag-bag for the purposes of this book. One thing I mean by the metaphysic of morals is an examination of the relation of moral judgement to other systems of concepts and to the facts of experience. The relation of thought to fact is, I think, the subject-matter of epistemology. But because there is dispute about what is and what is not to be counted as 'fact', epistemological discussion usually presupposes theories of ontology. And since ontological theories contain views about the relation between 'fact' and experience, epistemology often includes some psychological analysis. For my present purpose I have found it convenient not to try to keep rigidly separate questions of psychology, epistemology, and ontology.

I have also included in the second part of the book my attempt to unify the principles of moral obligation under the one principle of treating persons as ends, a task which might seem to fall more appropriately under the logic of morals. The reason why I have assigned it to the metaphysic of morals is that here the separation between my two problems cannot be maintained. In the logic of morals I am concerned with the relations between the intentional meanings of moral concepts, and I think that if we confine ourselves to intentional meaning we cannot systematize moral judgement to any further extent than is done by the deontologists. But if we consider what moral judgements presuppose, not merely what they say, we can suggest a further measure of coherence. In order to do this I have propounded a hypothesis of how the concept of moral obligation arises. This hypothesis cannot be securely tested against the intentional meaning of the concept as ordinarily used. It is a frankly speculative account, and I imagine there will be general agreement that speculation, if admitted to philosophy at all, had better be assigned to 'metaphysics' and not to 'logic'. Then those who prefer to confine their philosophical activities to the brass tacks of 'logic' can, if they wish, refuse the name of philosophy to speculation and metaphysics together. For my own part I am not afraid of the word 'metaphysics' or of speculative hypotheses. I think that philosophical and scientific progress is impossible without such hypotheses and the criticism which they invite. I have little confidence that my theory of moral obligation will be able to withstand criticism. But I hope that it may be found sufficiently interesting to provoke criticism and alternative suggestions in the light of such criticism. If it succeeds in doing that, I shall be well satisfied.

I take as the data of my inquiry the *reflective* moral judgements of ordinary life, and not the unreflective, habitual statements that we often make containing as elements the same *words* as reflective moral judgements. Many everyday statements containing the words 'ought', 'right', etc., are simply expressions of customs accepted without thinking and without any moral connotation. They are expressions, not of morals, but of what the anthropologists and sociologists call *mores*. 'You ought to raise your hat to a lady' implies no more than that it is customary in our society for men to show such acts (or better, relics) of chivalry to women, and that those who do not conform are frowned upon. In moral philosophy as I understand it, we are talking, not of *mores*, the slavish and unreflective following of customary habits of etiquette, of what is 'the done thing' in our society, but of what, when we reflect, we are prepared to stand by as right, irrespective of whether it is enjoined by custom or not. Customs or *mores* usually begin with a moral basis (e.g., the conventions of chivalry arose because it was and still is thought right to help and respect the weak, and because it was assumed in those days that women are a weaker sex), but they may come to outlive that moral basis and to remain with no genuine purpose. In such matters we are conservative, and we retain outworn customs so long as they do no great harm. Where changed circumstances make them a positive nuisance, reflective judgement says we ought (this is the moral 'ought') to scrap them. The data for moral philosophy, then, are those judgements containing moral words, which we stand by, if challenged, as stating what we really think is right or wrong. The distinction between moral and other norms is familiar enough to sociologists. For example, Professor M. Ginsberg, in his book *Reason and Unreason in Society*,[1] distinguishes the norms of 'law, religion, morality, convention, or fashion', and says that in developed civilizations it is usually easy to assign a given norm to one of these classes, though he rightly adds that it is not so easy to say precisely what constitutes the distinctions between them or why norms with apparently identical content

[1]p. 16.

are treated by different societies as belonging to different classes.

In the same book,[1] Professor Ginsberg gives his view of the distinction between moral philosophy and sociological treatments of morals.

> 'The psychology of the moral life . . . has long formed a part of the philosophical handling of ethical problems. Indeed there are ethical thinkers who regard ethics as consisting essentially in the history of moral development and the psychological analysis of moral approval and disapproval. To me, however, it seems clear that the psychology and sociology of morals must be definitely distinguished from ethics proper. Ethics must, of course, start with moral judgments as data, but in dealing with them its method should be critical in the Kantian sense. In other words, it should seek to elicit the assumptions latent in the judgments, the categories they employ, and in the light of this critical work to discover whether any fundamental principles can be formulated whereby actual morality could be made more coherent and systematic.'

I should not myself agree that all psychological discussion falls outside the philosophy of morals. The psychological analysis of moral experience is closely tied up with other analytical functions of the moral philosopher. The psychology of morals as a form of empirical science is concerned with moral behaviour as one among other kinds of publicly observable behaviour. For this purpose, 'moral behaviour' includes the utterance of moral judgements and the reporting of moral experience. The scientific treatment of moral judgement and experience, so regarded, is not the same as the psychological analysis undertaken, together with linguistic analysis, by the moral philosopher. The standpoint of the social scientist in dealing with the phenomena of morals is that of the external unimplicated observer, treating what he observes *'comme des choses'*, as Durkheim says. The moral philosopher considers

[1] p. 18.

the phenomena of morals from the standpoint of a person, a moral agent, he considers them as one potentially implicated in the sort of situation discussed; and this must involve taking account of moral experience as it presents itself to the moral agent. The psychological analysis of moral experience is especially important in a philosophical discussion of moral choice, but it must play some part also in a philosophical discussion of moral judgement.

Nevertheless, Professor Ginsberg's description of what he takes to be the whole task of moral philosophy corresponds pretty closely to what I have in mind as the main purpose of what I call the logic and metaphysic of moral judgement. It will be found that, like Ginsberg (and, in an earlier generation, Sidgwick, in his book *The Methods of Ethics*), I regard this task as the attempt to make more coherent and systematic the scheme of moral concepts and principles vaguely used in everyday life. It is not a mere description of usage. Beginning with description, it passes to linguistic recommendations in the interests of clarity. It pursues system not just for system's sake but in order to bring out more clearly what is the nature and purpose of moral judgement.

PART ONE

LOGIC OF MORALS

II

THE MEANING OF A LOGIC OF MORALS

In the logic of morals we are concerned with the system exhibited or implied by moral judgements. We have to examine the logical relationships to each other of moral concepts, e.g. whether goodness implies obligation or *vice versa*. Again, we have to consider the general principles of obligation and the relations between them, and to see if the system of interlocking principles thus constituted can be shown in a hierarchy of dependence. In short, the business of the logic of morals is to show the logical structure of the moral system (or of ethical language). '*The* moral system', I have said. But can we assume that there is only one such system (or 'language')? I answer that we cannot assume this, and indeed I shall suggest that the situation is similar to that with which we have now been made familiar in formal logic, namely that different systems can be constructed from different postulates and different definitions; to use the technical terminology of formal logic, we can produce alternative 'postulate sets'. The relation of the different sets to each other, and in what sense, if at all, one can be judged more true than, or superior to, its rivals, these are questions for the metaphysic of morals.

We begin, as I take it formal logic began, with the judgements of ordinary people in situations with which we are familiar. It may be that, in exhibiting the logic of such judgements, we are restricting ourselves to one particular system of morals, that which happens to be used in our particular civilization—just as it has been suggested, rightly or wrongly, that the logic of a language unrelated to the group of Indo-European languages is liable to be different from the Aristotelian logic. Or it may be that more than one moral system is embedded in our ordinary moral judgements. This was Sidgwick's conclusion from his examination of what he called the 'methods' of ethics. Indeed, our suggested study of the logic of morals is very close to what Sidgwick was doing. If we found such confusion of different systems in ordinary thought and language, we might then proceed beyond description to recommendation. We might clarify, extend, and modify, one of those systems, recommending its usage for application to all moral situations, as Sidgwick recommended the utilitarian 'method'. This may involve some re-defining of the primary terms or concepts employed, so as to ensure their inclusion in a single, interlocking system. Such construction of revised ethical language would not necessarily imply the hopeless aim of recommending that it be substituted in ordinary life for the more fluid and varied language now used. The recommendation would be primarily to fellow-philosophers, the suggestion being that such a clearer system of language would enable us the better to systematize moral thinking and bring out its presuppositions, throwing into greater relief the ultimate point of moral language.

It is conceivable that, instead of revising and refining the ethical language (or one of the ethical languages) found in use, we might invent a completely new one, a completely artificial language or symbolism, which would, when applied to moral situations, do even better the job of throwing into relief what is involved in morals. But I shall not attempt to fly so high.

Even if the system of ethics implied in the moral judgements of twentieth-century Europeans (or Britons) is different from that implied in the moral judgements of other civilizations, the task of exhibiting it clearly still has its intrinsic interest. Having completed that task, we should be prepared to consider the possibility of alternative systems and, in the metaphysic of morals, inquire if it is feasible to compare these different systems and attempt to rate one above another. The situation, as I see it, is similar to that in general logic, where we can exhibit formal relations within a system, consider the possibility or actual existence of alternative systems, and then, in 'philosophical logic' (or, as we might say, the metaphysic of logic) investigate the relations of the different systems to each other by an examination of their postulates and presuppositions.

In the logic of morals, then, we take as our primary data the moral judgements that are in fact made in ordinary life. We take them on trust as valid currency worth their nominal value, regardless of the possibility that an outside observer might think them counterfeit or over-valued. It is not part of the logic of morals to question whether we are justified in asserting what we do assert; that is a matter for the metaphysic of morals. We shall find, however, as in logic generally, that we have to go a little beyond what is written on the face of everyday judgements. For we must examine their implications, and, as in logic and mathematics, some of these implications are not immediately obvious. It is, I think, immediately obvious to the beginner in moral philosophy that 'ought' implies 'can'; he recognizes the truth of this when first put to him, although very likely he has not considered the matter before and so has not been explicitly aware of the implication. It is not immediately obvious whether an assertion that an act is right implies that it is the one which will produce the most good possible (though this would become an immediate implication in an artificially constructed system in which we *chose* to define rightness in terms of maximum attainable good). The clarification of these relationships between everyday moral judgements, then, is not simply the systematic stating of the obvious. It makes explicit what is barely implicit in everyday assertion. This perhaps involves from the start some measure of recommending, as the meaning of moral terms, fuller and more precise definitions than are present to the mind of the person using those terms in ordinary moral judgements. The more precise definitions will be necessary in order that the terms may be clearly shown to carry the implications which we say we are drawing out of them. But although we go beyond the relative vagueness of everyday judgement, we must not kick away the ladder on which we started. When we recommend more precise definitions from which implications will obviously follow, the implications must always be such as would commend themselves to ordinary moral reflection and such as do not violently conflict with ordinary moral judgements when applied to concrete situations. Otherwise our logic will not be applicable to moral thinking as it in fact goes on.

III

LOGIC OF MORAL PRINCIPLES

We want to clarify and refine the relationships between moral propositions, making explicit what is barely implicit in everyday moral judgements. The method of doing this is the one common to all systematization, the seeking out of general principles, and the rendering of these principles consistent both with each other and with the particular facts which they claim to cover. The first kind of consistency is the coherence of the system of general propositions. The second is accordance with the particular facts or data to which the system applies. In the field of ethics, the particular facts or data are the particular moral judgements of common sense made in concrete situations.

Coherence of the general propositions is tested in two ways, one negative, the other positive. The first gives us a weaker form of coherence, compatibility. The second gives us a tighter form, implication (or inclusion).

The negative test is the result of an attempt to prove inconsistency or incompatibility. We reach such a proof by showing that the two (or more) general propositions concerned lead, if held together, to self-contradiction. This is the familiar disproof of mathematics and logic, the *reductio ad absurdum*. Let us give an example. Suppose we contemplate admitting into our system the two general propositions:

(*a*) 'Our duty is always to realize the greatest possible good.'

(*b*) 'An agent is responsible for the doing or omission of his duty.'

These two propositions can be shown to be incompatible by drawing out some of their implications and producing a self-contradiction. Consider first proposition (*a*). We cannot know the total consequences of any action, and even with those that we may reasonably forecast we may make a mistake and find that the actual consequences belie our forecast or any reasonable forecast. So proposition (*a*) implies that we cannot ever know our duty (a conclusion drawn, e.g., by Professor Moore in *Principia Ethica*,[1] where he accepts something like proposition (*a*) as a definition of duty or right action). Turn now to proposition (*b*), which relates duty to responsibility. We impute responsibility only where an agent has knowledge or is in a position to acquire knowledge if he makes the effort; unavoidable ignorance takes away responsibility for an act. Proposition (*b*) asserts that a man is responsible for the doing or omission of his duty. It therefore implies that we can know what our duty is. Thus proposition (*a*) implies a proposition (*x*), 'We can never know what is our duty', and proposition (*b*) implies the contradictory of (*x*), 'We can know what is our duty'. (*a*) and (*b*) are therefore incompatible, in leading to mutually contradictory propositions.

What do we do if we find two principles incompatible with each other? We may reject one, retaining that which appears to be compatible with the remaining principles that we have provisionally admitted to our system. Or we may revise one or both of the two principles so that they cease to be incompatible. In our example, we can remove the inconsistency by modifying proposition (*a*) to

(*a*′) 'Our duty is always to realize the greatest *anticipated* good'.

If we do not find that two propositions held together lead to a self-contradiction, they are, so far as we can see at present, compatible. But of course we may have overlooked or failed to discover some of their implications which do render them incompatible; so that the negative method is not foolproof. We therefore seek, if possible, a more direct proof of coherence by the positive method; more direct, and foolproof, because it gives us the tighter kind of coherence, necessitation or inclusion, as against the looser coherence of compatibility.

The positive method is to show that the two propositions concerned are not merely compatible with each other but are necessarily connected, i.e. that one is implied by the other, or

[1] Ch. v.

that both are implied by a third, more-inclusive principle. Here are two simple pairs of examples to illustrate each of these possibilities.

We may have the two propositions:

(*c*) 'We ought to promote the increase of good.'

(*d*) 'We ought to promote the increase of pleasure.'

If we find that the word 'good' is used to refer to, let us say, virtue, love, pleasure, knowledge, and beauty, then (*d*) is included in, or implied by, (*c*).

Again, suppose we have the two propositions:

(*d*) 'We ought to promote the increase of pleasure.'

(*e*) 'We ought to promote the diminution of pain.'

We can show these to be necessarily connected if we take the third proposition

(*f*) 'We ought to satisfy desire',

and point out that the pursuit of pleasure and the avoidance of pain are each a species of what is desired. Thus (*d*) and (*e*) both follow from (*f*), and we can take (*f*) as the more-inclusive proposition. We should now be faced with the task of considering the relationship between (*c*) and (*f*).

I realize that the *truth* of some of the general propositions used in these simple examples may be questioned. In applying the tests of coherence we are merely assuming the truth of the general propositions whose logical relationships we are examining. Their truth is tested by the criterion of accordance with the moral judgements of common sense.

The positive method of testing coherence is, of course, more satisfying than the negative. For the positive test is not only foolproof against possible incompatibilities that might be found in the future; it also links our propositions together in such a way as to lead to a simpler, more generalized system of principles, the eventual hope being to find a single principle under which all the others fall.

Accordance of principles with the facts is likewise subject to both a positive and a negative test, the tests of a hypothesis. It is supported by pointing to particular moral judgements of common sense which conform to it; and (more important) it is upset by bringing a negative instance. For example, a hedonist might put forward the hypothesis that our sole duty is to maximize anticipated pleasure. We could criticize this by pointing to a situation where we think we ought to pay a debt although we are aware of an alternative possible action which we think would produce more pleasure. Our example shows the hypothesis to be inconsistent with some of the facts (ordinary moral judgements). We may remove the inconsistency by modifying the principle to the extent of abandoning its universality; i.e., we may modify it to: '*One* of our duties (or perhaps, our *chief* duty, the one most frequently encountered) is to maximize anticipated pleasure'. Our particular application of the test of discordance in this example has given us two principles in place of one: (1) the maximization of anticipated pleasure, (2) the payment of debts. Not that anyone would be satisfied with that as a system. Further tests, of coherence or accordance, will no doubt yield additional principles, and reduce one or other, and possibly both, of the two we now have, to some more-inclusive principle.

In testing coherence, the positive test was more satisfying than the negative. In testing accordance, the negative test is the more conclusive and the foolproof one, while the positive test of support by conforming instances always leaves a possible loop-hole for a negative instance to upset the universality of the hypothesis. This is a familiar distinction between *a priori* and empirical reasoning. The point to notice is that both apply in ethical systematization as in the system-making of an empirical science. Hypotheses, suggested general principles, are confirmed and disproved by empirical instances. When provisionally accepted into the system as general principles, they are subjected to the *a priori* tests of incompatibility and necessary connexion. The proposed system is an abstract logical schema which must try to satisfy the requirements of a deductive system, and at the same time it has to be applicable to the set of facts which it claims to systematize.

The situation is exactly the same as in an empirical science, i.e. the application of logical system or order to a set of facts.

The history of non-naturalistic theories of ethics is the history of attempts to exhibit a simple yet comprehensive system of the logic of morals. These attempts are criticized by the methods described above, and are modified in order to meet the criticisms. An example of the process can be seen in one of the main streams of British ethical theory. Egoistic hedonism, the theory that a man's sole duty is to maximize his own happiness, was widened into universalistic hedonism (or utilitarianism). In this wider theory we have two principles of duty, (1) the maximization of happiness (or anticipated happiness) for all persons whom we may affect by our action, and (2) the equal distribution of that happiness as between different persons. Bentham and Mill seemed to think that these two principles were necessarily connected, the second being implied by the first, but they failed to demonstrate this, and Sidgwick, whose theory is philosophically the best exposition of utilitarianism, kept the two principles separate. This system was criticized by Rashdall and Moore on the ground that the principle of maximizing happiness is insufficiently comprehensive; it does not accord, e.g., with the judgement that a society or world which contained a maximum of happiness but no knowledge or beauty, would leave much to be desired. They accordingly modified the system to 'ideal' or agathistic utilitarianism, in which the hedonistic utilitarians' principle of maximizing happiness was broadened into the principle of maximizing good, happiness being subsumed as a determinate form of good along with other determinates such as virtue, affection, beauty, and knowledge. As to the second principle of hedonistic utilitarianism, Moore seems to have forgotten all about it, but Rashdall attempted to subsume this, too, under the new comprehensive principle of maximizing good, justice being regarded, like happiness, as a determinate form of good. At this point we meet the criticism of deontologists that the scheme of the ideal utilitarians, no less than that of the hedonistic, fails to accord with judgements of duty that depend on a reference to the past; it does not account adequately for the duties of fulfilling contracts, of requiting desert, and of gratitude and reparation. Sir David Ross therefore sets out a system of duties in which a group of 'special obligations' is added to the 'general obligation' to produce as much good as possible. Hedonistic utilitarianism was criticized by ideal utilitarianism on the ground that the degree of goodness in a state of affairs is not determined solely by the degree of pleasure that it contains. Ideal utilitarianism was criticized on the ground that certain claims of justice do not depend simply on the amount of good realized. Both criticisms correctly assert that the system criticized fails to accord with the logic of everyday moral judgements. In the construction of a system that will cover common-sence moral judgements adequately, therefore, we must accept something like the one presented by the deontologists.

The great merit of the deontologists, Prichard, Ross, and Carritt (we may include also Richard Price who, in the eighteenth century, evolved a very similar theory),[1] is that they have carried out a meticulous analysis of the implications of common-sense moral judgements, and have kept close to those judgements in their theoretical systems. They have had foremost in their attention the test of accordance with such judgements, and have been cautious of leaping too quickly ahead with the positive test of coherence, that is, with the attempt to unify their systems under a single, allegedly all-inclusive, principle. At the same time they have done painstaking work with the negative test of coherence, that is, with drawing out the implications of moral concepts and principles so as to show incompatibilities in loosely framed statements of principles, and thus they have shown the necessity of careful reformulation of such concepts and principles so as to remove the in-

[1]H. A. Prichard, *Moral Obligation;* W. D. Ross, *The Right and the Good,* and *Foundations of Ethics;* E. F. Carritt, *The Theory of Morals,* and *Ethical and Political Thinking;* Richard Price, *A Review of the Principal Questions in Morals.*

consistencies. The outstanding example of this is their discussion of duty in relation to knowledge,[1] in consequence of which they have distinguished between 'objective', 'subjective', and 'putative' duty.

They have also given us classifications of types of duty. Sir David Ross and Dr. Carritt classify duties both at a less general, and at a more general, level. Richard Price had previously given a list of six 'main and leading branches of Virtue'[2], which corresponds to the less general level of classification in the systems of Ross and Carritt. When we compare the systems of these three philosophers, we find that although they cover pretty much the same ground, their lists of principles do not altogether coincide. This is true even at the less general level of classification, where each writer gives about half-a-dozen principles. Their lists overlap to a considerable extent, but there are divergences. One of the three philosophers will link principles (*a*) and (*b*) (say, promoting the happiness of others, and promoting their virtue) together, and will keep principle (*c*) (say, refraining from injury) separate from the former.[3] Another will link (*a*) and (*c*), and separate (*b*).[4] Again, Ross suggests[5] that the duty of veracity is to be subsumed as a determinate form of the duty to keep promises, while Price reverses the subsumption, saying that veracity is the less specific principle and promise-keeping a determinate form of that.[6] These divergences, even at the less general level of systematization, show that the system of principles employed by common sense is not clear cut and obvious. In attempting to set it out, the deontological philosophers have to make it more tidy than it appears in ordinary moral thinking, and accordingly they have to interpret, to some extent, the

[1]Prichard, *Moral Obligation*, essay 2; Ross, *Foundations of Ethics*, ch. vii; Carritt, *Ethical and Political Thinking*, ch. ii. Cf. Price, *Review of Morals*, ch. viii.

[2]*Review of Morals*, ch. vii.

[3]Cf. Ross, *The Right and the Good*, p. 21.

[4]Cf. Carritt, *Ethical and Political Thinking*, pp. 106-7.

[5]Loc. cit.

[6]*Review of Morals* (my edition), p. 155.

implications carried within the system. They differ in their interpretations, and it cannot be said with any assurance that one of their three systems is a more accurate interpretation of common-sense moral thinking than the others. Where they differ from each other, each of the divergent interpretations seems to fit common-sense judgements with reasonable adequacy.

Now the stock criticism of deontological theories of ethics is that they leave us with 'an unconnected heap' of obligations.[1] Such a theory may be less vulnerable to criticism on the score of discordance with common-sense judgements than is a (supposedly) simpler system like utilitarianism or agathism. But this, the critics may say, is just because the deontological system is less tidy, being hardly a system at all; that is, it has a low degree of coherence, at least in the tighter sense of coherence as necessary connexion and subsumption of principles under more general ones. To this criticism deontologists may reply: 'But if the system exhibited in common-sense judgements is complex and loosely coherent, we must not try to over-simplify it. Simplicity at the expense of comprehensiveness, coherence at the expense of accordance with fact, means paying too high a price for the desired article.'

Yet the article is desired. The deontologists do pursue coherence to a certain extent, and do depart from common-sense moral judgements at least when these have a vagueness leading to incompatibilities. At their face value, common-sense moral judgements are incoherent not only in the sense of not being necessarily connected, of forming an unrelated heap, but also, to some degree, in the other sense of leading to incompatibilities. The deontologists, after bringing out those incompatibilities, as we have noted, have then proceeded to refine the language and concepts of morals so as to remove the incompatibilities. In ordinary language we do not distinguish explicitly between the idea of duty as the requirement to do what is objectively right, and the idea of duty as the requirement to do what the agent thinks right. Nor do we make any

[1]Cf. H. W. B. Joseph, *Some Problems in Ethics*, e.g., p. 67.

distinction between a 'duty' and an 'obligation' (or a '*prima facie* duty'); that distinction of usage is propounded by the deontologists in order to resolve the self-contradiction implied in talk of a 'conflict of duties' (for a duty must be within the agent's power, and two conflicting proposed actions are not both within the agent's power). If, in the interests of coherent theory, and indirectly in the interests of clearer thinking in practical moral judgements, we are prepared to alter, or at least refine, the language and concepts of common sense, why should we not, in the interests of theory, go farther and seek the tighter coherence of an interlocking system?

Indeed, the different, though overlapping, schemes of the deontologists show that, while common-sense judgements vaguely imply a system on these lines, they give no clear guide for classification even at the less general level of half-a-dozen principles. In their systems, even at this level, the deontologists have gone farther in positive coherence than common-sense thinking does, and their lack of coherence with each other shows that we must go farther still. At least, this follows unless we are prepared to abandon systematization altogether and remain what Sidgwick called 'perceptional intuitionists',[1] holding the view that each particular judgement of duty is related only to its own situation and cannot be classified with others. But this position is unwarranted by common-sense judgements themselves, which often describe a particular action as being a duty in virtue of some characteristic (e.g., relieving distress, or keeping a promise) which it shares with other obligatory acts. That is to say, common-sense moral thinking and discourse do frequently bear out the sort of theory that the deontologists give us in their lower-level degree of systematization. It seems to me, for the reasons I have given, that we cannot stop there but must attempt a further degree of systematization. And in fact, some of the deontologists do take the step of further systematization; for Sir David Ross and Dr. Carritt tentatively suggest more

[1] *The Methods of Ethics*, Book I, ch. viii.

generalized groupings of their half-dozen principles under two or three wider principles. We may note, too, that Ross prefaces his suggestion with the remark that his earlier catalogue of half-a-dozen principles (what I have called the lower-level system) makes no claim to being ultimate. 'If further reflection discovers a perfect logical basis for this or for a better classification, so much the better.'[1]

The two principles of Sir David Ross's generalized scheme[2] are as follows: (1) The general duty to produce good and avoid evil. (Under this are subsumed the less general principles of duty that enjoin the promotion of justice, beneficence, and self-improvement, and the avoidance of injuring others.) (2) The category of special duties to particular persons. (Under this are subsumed the principles of duty that enjoin gratitude, reparation, and the fulfilment of contracts.) Dr. Carritt[3] gives three main principles of duty: (1) Justice (sub-divided into distributive, retributive, and restitutive), (2) Improvement, i.e. the increase of good and decrease of evil, (3) Beneficence, i.e. the increase of happiness and the decrease of unhappiness. Carritt separates (2) and (3) because he doubts whether happiness is, as such, good, and if it is not, the undoubted duty to increase happiness must be regarded as unconnected with the duty to increase good. But even so, it is plain that (2) and (3) are of a similar type as contrasted with the duties of justice, and if we were to use the equivocal word 'beneficence' to cover both the production of good and the production of happiness, we could say that Dr. Carritt's scheme consists of two main principles, justice and beneficence.

If we compare the more generalized classifications proposed by Ross and Carritt, we see that these, like their less general catalogues, do not coincide with each other. Nor do they coincide with the utilitarian systems of similar level of generality, and yet in some respects they follow the same lines as the utilitarian schemes. The different general systems of the deon-

[1] *The Right and the Good*, p. 23.
[2] Ibid., pp. 24 ff.
[3] *Ethical and Political Thinking*, ch. ix.

tologists, like their different lower-level systems, seem to be alternative possibilities. We may be able to bring forward some considerations that would favour one of the alternatives, but so far as common-sense moral judgements go the different groupings seem equally permissible.

Sidgwick gave the name of 'dogmatic intuitionism' to a theory which, unlike 'perceptional intuitism', classified duties under a number of principles. Dogmatic intuitionism, he held, gives a correct picture of the reflective moral thinking of common sense. But because of the incoherence of the various principles in such a theory, Sidgwick considered that a moral theorist cannot rest satisfied with dogmatic intuitionism but must proceed to a 'philosophical intuitionism' in which the different principles are rendered coherent. He regarded his own brand of utilitarianism as a form of 'philosophical intuitionism'. It seems to me that while Sidgwick's general programme is persuasive, his particular application of it takes the wrong direction. Now Kant's theory of ethics, which is on deontological lines, attempts to unify the various principles of duty in his formulations of a single 'Categorical Imperative'. If we were to use Sidgwick's terminology, Kant could be described as a 'philosophical intuitionist'. Despite the criticisms of detail that suggest themselves, Kant's unified theory impresses almost all his readers as bringing out something important and true. We could not say that common-sense moral judgement has at the surface of consciousness any of Kant's formulations of the Categorical Imperative, yet many if not most of us feel that Kant somehow expresses what is fundamental to morality, the morality implied in ordinary moral judgements.

Reflection on the moral judgements of common sense, and on the history of philosophical discussion of these, leads to a system of moral principles of the kind set out by the deontologists. Such a system gives a correct picture of the logic of moral principles as employed in reflective moral judgement. The moral philosopher, however, cannot rest content with that, but must attempt to unify the system. My view is that some parts of Kant's theory give the most promising lead for this task. But since the result of such unification discloses, not what is present to the moral consciousness of common sense in its reflective judgements, but the presuppositions of such judgements, the unified theory belongs to the metaphysic of morals.

IV

LOGIC OF MORAL CONCEPTS

§1. *On defining ethical terms*

In the construction of a logical system, the relations of key concepts, no less than of key propositions, to each other need to be specified. Simplicity in the system is contributed by defining some of the concepts in terms of others, which are then the basic or 'primitive' concepts of the system. Professor Moore makes 'good' the key concept of his system in *Principia Ethica,* and defines 'right' and duty' (and, by implication, other ethical concepts) in terms of 'good'. The deontologists point out that such a system fails to accord with certain classes of moral judgements, and they therefore regard 'ought' (or 'right') and 'good' as both irreducible concepts. Dr. Ewing has suggested the idea of 'fitting' as a single fundamental concept, in terms of which 'good', 'right', and 'duty', may be defined.

All these suggestions are made within a so-called intuitionist or non-naturalist theory of ethics, that is, a theory which (1) denies the possibility of reducing ethical terms to non-ethical, and (2) accordingly holds that ethical terms stand for peculiar characteristics the presence of which is attested, not by the senses or feeling, but by intellectual intuition. The latter half of this contention concerns a metaphysical and an epistemological (in appearance, a psychological) problem, with which we shall be concerned in Part II. The former half of the contention, that ethical terms are not reducible to non-ethical, deals with a logical problem, the possibility or impossibility of substituting one kind of term for another to serve the purposes of the language of ethics. Needless to say, the two problems are not unconnected, and if the second half of the non-naturalists' contention is true the first half will follow. But the converse does not hold. If it be true that ethical terms cannot be satisfactorily replaced by non-ethical to serve the purposes in fact served by ethical language, this does not necessarily imply that ethical terms stand for objects or characteristics that could not, in a different context, be correctly described by non-ethical terms.

Attempts to 'define' ethical concepts in terms of non-ethical have met with two types of difficulty. The first may equally meet non-naturalistic definitions, i.e. definitions of one ethical concept in terms of another. The suggested definition may fail to be identical in denotation with the concept to be defined. A theorist wishing to be rid of specifically ethical terms, because he objects to the suggestion that there is a peculiar realm of ethical objects different from the natural, may, if he chooses, construct an arbitrary system with arbitrary definitions and stick to them. If he chooses to mean, whenever he uses the word 'good', nothing more and nothing less than, say, pleasant, who is to stop him? (Better still, in order to avoid confusion in communication with others, whose usage does not accord with his proposal, he can drop the word 'good' altogether and simply use the word 'pleasant'.) But if our aim is to discover the logic of the ethical language at present in use, we cannot adopt so arbitrary a procedure. If we start off by defining 'good', e.g. in the manner of Hobbes, as any object of the speaker's desire, we can construct a system, but, for the purpose of understanding the current usage of 'good', it will be a limited and incomplete system that fails to denote all that is denoted by ordinary use of the word.

Further, unless we can remember to dispense throughout with ordinary usages of ethical words, we are liable to find that the arbitrary definitions of our key concepts lead to inconsistencies with the implications of those ordinary usages into which we naturally slip, thus producing inconsistencies in our system. This difficulty is apparent in the philosophy of Hobbes, and it forms the gist of *a priori* criticisms of him such as those made by Samuel Clarke; most of Clarke's criticisms of Hobbes can be boiled down to the single criticism that

Hobbes's system contains inconsistencies between his initial definitions of ethical terms and some of his uses, corresponding to everyday uses, of those terms within the body of the system. Such criticisms can be met by revising the language used in the system so as to render it all consistent with the initial definitions. Thus it is possible to revise Hobbes's language where he lapses into ordinary usage, so as to produce a consistent system of Hobbesian ethics. The system will then be consistent, but it will be arbitrary; it will fail to accord with ordinary usage and so will not represent the system implied in the moral judgements of common sense. *A posteriori* criticism of Hobbes, such as that posed by Butler, draws attention to the discordances between the Hobbesian system and common sense.

Yet a naturalistic system which did not suffer from such discordance could still perhaps be evolved. It might begin with tentative definitions such as those of Hobbes, discover their limitations and defects by use of the tests of coherence and accordance, and then modify the tentative definitions so as to try to remove the faults. Having discovered that, e.g., Hobbes's definition of 'good' as 'the object of the speaker's desire' is insufficiently comprehensive, we might modify it, e.g. to 'the object of anyone's desire', so as to make it accord more adequately with the data of common-sense judgements, until at the end we might reach a definition that did accord with the data.

But now there arises the second type of objection to naturalistic definitions of ethical terms, namely that, even where they coincide in denotation with the ordinary usage of ethical terms, they fail to coincide in connotation. This criticism is posed in the test used notably by Richard Price and Professor Moore[1] for the adequacy of a definition. Their test of a definition was to see whether the proposition formed by making the definition subject and the definiendum predicate, is a tautology. For example, if the word 'good' is defined as the object of desire, we form the proposition 'The object of desire is

[1]Price, *Review of Morals*, ch. i; Moore, *Principia Ethica*, ch. i.

good', and ask whether this is a tautology in the trivial sense in which 'The object of desire is the object of desire' is a tautology. If the proposition is not a tautology in this trivial sense, the proposed definition is faulty, for it is not identical in 'meaning' (i.e. connotation) with the definiendum.

Price and Moore used this test only for proposed definitions of ethical words (Price used it for 'right', Moore for 'good') in terms of non-ethical words. But it may be applied equally to *any* proposed definition, to definitions of non-ethical words in non-ethical terms, and to definitions of ethical words in ethical terms.[1] And the trouble with the test is that it allows very few definitions to pass through its mesh. Most commonly accepted definitions—e.g., 'Man is a rational animal', 'A straight line is the shortest distance between two points'—are not tautologies in the sense required by Price and Moore. When we normally use the word 'man' the idea we have before our minds is not identical with the idea we have before our minds when we use the expression 'rational animal'; the idea expressed by 'man' is both vaguer and, usually, wider than that expressed by 'rational animal'. The only definitions, apart from mere synonyms, that will pass the test are those in which it is immediately obvious that the analysis given as the definition is an implication of the term to be defined, an implication which is at the threshold of consciousness when we ordinarily use the definiendum. This is true of Professor Moore's example[2] of a sound definition, 'A brother is a male sibling' (provided we happen to know the word 'sibling'). But it is not true of most accepted definitions, and the reason is simple. Moore's type of definition, stating an obvious implication of the definiendum, is of little use for the purposes for which definitions are normally required. The position of the naturalist in ethics is little shaken by an argument that says, in effect, 'Your proposed definitions of ethical words will not do, because practically no definitions of any words will do'. The objection is to the practice of defining, not to a doctrine about the nature of

[1]Cf. W. K. Frankena, 'The Naturalistic Fallacy', *Mind,* October, 1939.
[2]In his 'Reply to my Critics', *The Philosophy of G. E. Moore,* p.664.

ethical terms. '*Everything* is what it is, and not another thing', and in the light of Moore's use of his test of a definition we may re-phrase his motto as 'Every word (or, if he prefers it, every concept) is what it is, and not another word'. The objection is to the 'defining' of 'good' and almost anything else, owing to Moore's narrowly restricted, and arbitrary, use of 'definition'. If the naturalist ceases to talk of 'definition', and says instead that the word 'good' is used to express, or denote, or refer to, the object of desire (or whatever else he has espoused as the 'meaning' of 'good'), the objection does not touch him.

Now Price and Moore thought that the successful use of their test against proposed naturalistic definitions of ethical words proved that the primary concept of ethics is a 'simple idea' or an 'unanalysable quality'. Why should they have thought this? If you were to offer me an unsatisfactory definition of 'brother', and if I showed it to be unsatisfactory by the use of Moore's test, I should not thereby have proved that no correct definition, even in Moore's sense of definition, could be given. The argument underlying Moore's thought is presumably that, since people have been suggesting definitions of 'good' for centuries, and since all these definitions fail the test, it is most unlikely that a correct definition still lies waiting to be discovered. On Moore's view of definition, this would indeed be most unlikely; for a definition that satisfied his test would be an analysis which is immediately seen to be obviously implied by the definiendum, and such an obvious implication could hardly remain undiscovered in the course of centuries of brain-racking. Even so, does failure to produce a satisfactory definition prove that the definiendum is unanalysable, that it is 'simple' or has no distinguishable parts? If that were true, the test would 'prove' simplicity in cases where a correct *partial* analysis of the definiendum had been given and was found, on application of the test, to be an unsatisfactory definition. For instance, suppose 'a cause' (in the sense in which we speak of one event causing another) is defined as an event of a type that invariably precedes an event of another type, called the effect. This definition does not satisfy Moore's test. It is not a tautology to say that an event of a type that invariably precedes an event of another type is the cause of the second event; for, as Hume himself recognized, the definiendum, 'cause', contains also the notion of necessary connexion with its effect. But it does not follow from the failure of this and other suggested definitions of 'cause', that the notion of 'cause' is unanalysable or simple. The trouble with the proposed definition is not that it attempts to analyse the parts of something that has no parts, but that it gives an incomplete analysis; it specifies certain parts of the notion to be analysed, but omits another part. Failure over a long period of trying to give a correct definition may suggest that a correct definition, in Moore's sense of definition, is impossible, but it does not show that the definiendum is a simple idea.

Indeed the whole conception of simple and complex ideas, derived from Locke's faulty *psychology* of perception, may be misleading as a criteriological dichotomy for the logical business of definition. When 'man' is defined as 'rational animal', this does not mean that a man consists of two parts, one an animal, the other a rational something added to the animal. The definition means that a man is (wholly) an animal but is distinguished from other animals by being rational. The 'analysis' is not in the least analogous, as Moore claims it should be, to specifying the parts of a horse, 'four legs, a head, a heart, a liver, etc., etc.'[1] It may be replied that rational and animal are parts, not of a man, but of the concept or idea of man. But in what sense is a non-spatial entity supposed to have parts? The definition uses two terms instead of one, or, if you like, expresses two ideas instead of one. But a psychologically simple idea, such as the idea of yellow, can be 'defined', in a perfectly proper use of the word 'defined', by a phrase which employs more than one term, or expresses more than one idea, e.g. 'that colour which is midway in the spectrum between orange and green'. (Philosophers holding the traditional view of definition *per genus et differentiam* could of course object

[1]*Principia Ethica*, p. 8.

that my example involves extending the application of the term *differentia* beyond the customary usage. But Moore's view of definition, as analysis into parts, is not the traditional one, and therefore criticism of him need not be narrowly confined to the traditional standpoint.)

When Price and Moore use their test to reject naturalistic definitions of ethical words, they have in mind something different from a narrowing criterion of definition in general. Their point is that any proposed definition of an ethical concept in non-ethical terms seems to leave out something, something that can only be expressed in ethical language. The point of saying that we can always ask significantly of any natural entity or combination of natural entities whether it is good, is that 'good' seems to express an idea quite different from that expressed by any word referring to an existing or possibly existing thing. What Price and Moore wish to emphasize about ethical terms is better stated by contrasting 'fact' with 'value', or better still, 'is' with 'ought'. And that way of posing the point has been most clearly seen and taken by the naturalist Hume.[1]

When thus stated, the force of the argument has been recognized by modern naturalists. They no longer give descriptive definitions of ethical words, according to which these words would *state* the existence of natural objects or characteristics. Instead, they hold that the function of ethical words is different from the function of descriptive words; sentences containing ethical words have the force of ejaculations or commands, not the force of statements. In its proper place, and shorn of its exaggerations, this theory brings out an important element in the nature of ethical language. But it will not do as an account of the logic of ethical terms. So far as the logic of morals is concerned, sentences containing ethical words purport to be statements, and are commonly taken as such by plain men using them in everyday life. That they usually have, in addition, an expressive or imperative force, need not be denied, for that is true of many other statements, though

[1] *Treatise of Human Nature*, Book III, Part I, section i, last paragraph.

perhaps not often to the same degree. But when a man says 'I think I ought to do so-and-so', he expresses a belief that something is the case, and when he asks himself whether he ought to do something he is posing a question which he thinks is to be answered by a statement. The significance, for the logic of morals, of the 'expressive' or imperative' version of naturalism, as opposed to the 'descriptive', lies in the recognition by naturalists that ethical words cannot be translated by words descriptive of the natural world, that 'ought' and 'is' belong to different modes of speech.

The argument of Price and Moore about attempted naturalistic definitions of ethical words does not prove that such words are indefinable. It is a fence to keep us within the boundary of ethical language or the ethical category. The 'meaning' or connotation of ethical terms can only be expressed in the ethical language. It may well be that the denotation of such words can be correctly described, but with a different force of connotation, in non-ethical language; it may well be that the meaning of, say, 'object of desire', runs parallel with the meaning of 'good'. But the logic of ethical words must be confined within the ethical language. Ethical words have *logical* relations with each other; we can, without committing the 'heterogeneous fallacy' (as Dr. Carritt[1] re-names the 'naturalistic fallacy'), consider the possibility of defining one ethical term by means of another, and whether one is implied by another. Ethical terms do not have such logical relations with non-ethical terms. There may well be other kinds of invariable relation between ethical and non-ethical terms. Almost every intuitionist admits as much. Intuitionists have commonly agreed that what is good always includes pleasure, and is always approvable by the person calling it good. But such relations are not a matter of logic. The argument of Price and Moore shows us that we use ethical terms in a linguistic system of their own, that we think of ethical concepts as occupying a category of their own.

It does not necessarily follow that ethical terms refer to

[1]*Ethical and Political Thinking*, p. 13.

peculiar entities of which we become aware by a peculiar faculty. That view depends on a particular theory of knowledge and a particular ontology underlying that epistemology. Just as the empiricists' particular theory of knowledge, with its underlying ontology, has led to rash conclusions about the logic of moral judgements, so the sounder logical treatment of the non-naturalists may lead to rash conclusions about the epistemology of morals. Each of these two issues needs to be discussed in its proper place and with arguments relevant to its own domain. Naturalists, no less than non-naturalists, have hailed Moore's argument as supporting their epistemological theories. In fact the argument relates to the logic of morals, and to that alone. It is a warning to keep the logic of morals separate from questions of epistemology, psychology, and ontology.

§2. *Obligation and goodness*

Let us begin with the suggestion that 'ought' and 'good' should be taken as the two basic concepts of our system. Can either of these two be eliminated as a primitive notion, so that our logic of moral concepts may be based on a single concept? In order to eliminate one of the two, we must either define it in terms of the other together with some non-ethical notion, or else be able to define it or adequately translate it by some non-ethical notion alone. Moore's test shows that the latter expedient will not work for those uses of the words 'ought' and 'good' that we feel to be 'specifically ethical'. But it does work for other, 'non-ethical', uses of these words.

There are situations in which we say 'That's good', where we might be willing to allow that we mean hardly more than 'I like that' or 'That satisfies a need'; for instance, if we drink a cup of tea after a long walk and say 'Ah, that's good'. But in what we feel to be 'specifically ethical' uses, the word 'good' has a peculiar connotation which cannot be translated by words describing psychological states.

The so-called categorical use of the word 'ought' likewise

has a peculiarly ethical connotation and cannot be translated by non-ethical terms. In what is called the hypothetical use of the word 'ought', we are often willing to allow that our meaning can be translated by non-ethical terms. It should be noted, however, that these non-ethical terms include reference not only to causation, or means and ends, but also to a notion of the practical requirements of consistency,[1] a notion that perhaps cannot be called naturalistic. For example, 'You ought to take your medicine' means something like this: 'Taking medicine will cause you to get better, and since you want to get better the realization of that purpose implies, if your actions are to be consistent with your adopted purposes, a requirement that you start the necessary causal chain'. (The non-moral 'ought', as an imperative of consistency in action, is akin to the logical imperative of consistency in thought, which requires us, if we accept the premisses of an argument, to accept the conclusion implied by them. We 'ought', or are logically 'bound', though not psychologically determined, to accept the conclusion. The word 'ought' is occasionally transferred from the 'logical imperative' to describe logical implication itself, e.g. in the sentence 'If this train is running to time, we ought to be approaching the Forth Bridge'. Here the expression 'we ought to be approaching' simply means 'it follows that we are approaching'; the 'ought' states a logical consequence alone, and does not express a requirement on any person to initiate some action.)

Alternatively, some uses of the 'hypothetical' sense of 'ought' can be translated into a combination of the ethical term 'good' (instead of, or in addition to, the non-ethical concept of desire) with the notions of causation and practical requirement. For instance, if I say 'You ought to see the current performance of Goethe's *Faust*', I may have in mind not only the probability that you will enjoy the experience but also the thought that such an experience is intrinsically good. When Professor Moore said that 'right' means 'cause of a good result',

[1]Cf. Sidgwick, *The Methods of Ethics* (7th edition), p. 37; C. D. Broad, *Five Types of Ethical Theory*, pp. 162-3.

this was true of some uses of the 'hypothetical' meaning of 'right'.

Some senses of the word 'good', and one of the hypothetical uses of the word 'ought', then, do not belong to the specifically ethical language. We are still left with ethical uses of both terms. Can we simplify our system by making one of the two terms, in their ethical use, the basic one and defining the other by means of it? For example, can we say that the second type of hypothetical 'ought' mentioned above, in which the word may be translated by a combination of 'good' and non-ethical terms, is identical with the moral or so-called categorical use of 'ought'? This is the view adopted by Professor Moore in *Principia Ethica,* when he defined 'ought' as 'useful' or 'causing a good result'. He in effect denied that there is any non-hypothetical use of 'ought' or 'right'. A system can indeed be built up in this way, but it does not accord with the system in use. Some of the propositions implied by such a system are at variance, not only in meaning, but in material effect, with the moral judgements that most men would make in certain situations.

Nor can 'good', in all its ethical uses, be defined in terms of 'ought'. It might, for instance, be suggested that 'good' can be defined as what one ought to pursue. But this proposal, too, would discord with some of the judgements of common sense. There are some things which we should call good while yet not thinking that we ought to realize them or the opportunity for them. For example, self-sacrifice for the removal of evil is good; if the evil is there, we think that the self-sacrifice involved in overcoming it is good, and that its goodness outweighs the evil that it opposes. Yet we should not therefore think it right to produce the evil conditions and thereupon the good of self-sacrifice to outweigh them. Nor, even when the evils are already there, do we necessarily think it a *duty* to sacrifice self in order to overcome them, for we regard some virtue as going beyond what duty requires and yet as undoubtedly good and that to a high degree.

One type of goodness (or one ethical sense of the word

'good'), however, is definable in terms of duty. When we call a man morally good we sometimes mean that he has acted, or that he usually acts, as he ought and from the thought that he ought to do the action, or actions, in question. (Perhaps we should add that this use of 'good' may also involve the idea that the man deserves praise and happiness. We must consider later whether the notion of desert has to be admitted as a further basic ethical concept, or whether it can be translated either in non-ethical terms or in terms of an ethical notion already admitted.) In order to isolate this sense of 'good' or type of goodness, we may decide to restrict the expression 'morally good' to this kind of goodness, and to call other types of virtue 'excellence (ἀρετή) of character'. Already, it will be noted, we begin to refine and sharpen the ethical language beyond ordinary usage. But in this linguistic recommendation we do not contradict the material decisions of ordinary moral judgement.

Our conclusion so far is this. One sense of 'ought' or 'right' is definable in non-ethical terms or in a combination of non-ethical terms and 'good'; another sense of 'ought' is not so definable. One ethical sense of 'good', namely moral goodness, may be translated in terms of the moral 'ought' (and perhaps of desert, which itself requires consideration); another ethical sense of 'good', namely intrinsic good other than moral good, is not so translatable. We have therefore eliminated, from our basic concepts of the ethical system, certain senses of the words 'ought' and 'good', but we are still left with two independent ethical notions, the idea of moral or 'categorical' obligation, and the idea of non-moral, intrinsic good.

§3. *Duties and rights*

We have accepted the 'deontological' view that the moral use of 'ought' is a basic concept that cannot be derived from the idea of goodness. We must now introduce language that will enable us to distinguish between the incumbency of a proposed action as exemplifying a moral principle, and the incumbency of a proposed action as being judged, amid a conflict of possible actions each exemplifying a moral principle, to be paramount. Let us call the first 'obligation', and the second 'duty'. In the usage we are proposing, 'obligation' is equivalent to our primary concept of 'ought'; 'duty' means either (1) an obligation in the absence of conflicting obligations, or (2) the obligation judged, amid a conflict of obligations, to be paramount. The word 'judged' in the second half of our definition of duty is deliberately vague. Judged by whom? By the agent? Or by some other person or persons? There is room for difference of opinion on this issue, which involves the tangled problem of the 'subjective' or 'objective' ground of duty. My own opinion on this issue is that the ground of duty, amid a conflict of obligations, is usually the judgement of the agent but sometimes the judgement of other persons. My definition, while leaving the question open to some degree, is phrased so as to allow for the view I shall propose.

We turn next to the notion of rights. There are, I think, two senses of the word 'right' used as a noun. First, 'I have a right to do an action' (or a series of actions, as when I say that I have a right to use my property as I wish), means 'I have no duty to refrain from so acting'. It is usually presupposed, when I make such a statement, that I want or propose to do the action in question, and I should not normally use this form of statement unless it had been suggested that there was some moral or legal obstacle to my following my wishes or intentions. In this sense, 'I have a right' asserts a *nihil obstat* to the carrying out of a proposed action. There is, however, a second use of 'I have a right', in which I describe the same fact as I describe by saying that someone else has a duty to me. 'I have a right to the money Jones owes me' describes the same fact as 'Jones has a duty to pay me the money he owes'. The first kind of a right is a right to act; to say that one has such a right is to say that the proposed action is not wrong, there is no duty to refrain from doing the action. The second kind of a right is a right against someone else, a right to receive something; to say that one has such a right is to say that someone else has a duty to the person described as having the right. We might call the first kind 'a right of action',[1] and the second kind 'a right of recipience'.

Whenever I have a right of action, I also have a right of recipience of a particular kind. If I have a *nihil obstat* right, or a right of action, to stand on my head, I also have the second kind of right not to be prevented from exercising my right of action. That is to say, where there is no moral obstacle to my fulfilling a desire, there is a moral obstacle to interference by others with my pursuit of my purpose. The reason for this is that there is always an obligation not to hinder other persons in their fulfilment of their desires provided that their pursuit of such purposes is not itself wrong. By saying that a man has a right of action to do what he wishes, we are saying that there is nothing wrong, he contravenes no obligation, in pursuing his purpose. Accordingly there is something wrong, it is a contravention of an obligation, for other people to interfere with his pursuit of his permissible purpose. This right of recipience against others that they do not interfere with the exercise of one's rights of action, is the right of social liberty. There are, of course, many other kinds of rights of recipience, or rights against others; that is, there are many other kinds of rights which describe the duties of others towards the person said to have rights against them.

We have defined both uses of the noun 'right' in terms of 'ought'. In the first sense of a right, when we say a man has a right we mean that he has no duty to refrain from a proposed action; in the second sense, we mean that someone else has a duty to him. In virtue of the second definition, the two forms of expression '*A* has a duty to *B*' and '*B* has a right (of recipience) against *A*' are correlative in the sense of analytic-

[1]Not to be confused with the technical term of English Law, 'a right of action', which means a right to take *legal* action to have implemented a claim against another, i.e. to enforce the securing of what I am here calling a right of recipience.

ally implying each other. They may not be connotatively tautologous in ordinary speech, though they are so in the more precise language which we are here recommending. But it can be claimed that the more precise usage proposed involves sharper precision only and not a definite alteration of meaning.

Since we are distinguishing, in our language, between duties and obligations, we must likewise introduce suitable terms to make the distinction at the other side of the 'ought' relation. We shall call the correlative of a duty a 'right', and the correlative of an obligation a 'claim'. A claim bears the same relation to a right as an obligation bears to a duty. That is, in the absence of conflicting principles, an obligation implies a duty and a claim implies a right, while in the presence of conflicting principles, being judged the strongest obligation implies being a duty, and being judged the strongest claim implies being a right. All these implications are analytic, they follow from the definitions we have introduced.

We have, then, made a tidy enough beginning for our logic of the term 'ought'. We have used it as the basic term for defining others in such a way that the terms introduced have a relatively high degree of coherence, of analytic implications, with each other. The implications are trivial but they enable us to employ the terms 'obligation', 'duty', 'claim', right', pretty widely, as Dr. Carritt particularly (and to some extent Sir David Ross, though with slightly different terminology) has employed them. The value of a system of logical rules is not to be judged by the complexity of the rules. A few very simple rules can have a wide and varied application in use. The rules of chess are relatively few and simple; the number of moves and chess-board situations that they permit is immense.

But will our tidy little scheme do the job which it is intended to do, will it apply to all situations where in ordinary life we talk of duties and rights? There are four types of instance in which it seems difficult to say that duties imply rights, or obligations imply claims. Is it justifiable to link these pairs of notions so closely as we have done, or must we say that rights and claims are not simply logically equivalent to (i.e. implying and implied by) duties and obligations?

(*a*) It is commonly thought that at any rate *one* principle of obligation, if not the sole principle as claimed by ideal utilitarianism, is the obligation to realize good. But since the obligation is to realize good abstractly and not the good of someone, there is no person to have a claim against the agent who is obliged. His obligation is not to a particular person or to a group of persons; it is not *to* anyone.

(*b*) Some of our obligations to persons are what are sometimes called 'duties of supererogation' or 'duties of imperfect obligation'. If a man performs such acts (e.g. of charity), we praise him and say he has done what is right and good. But if he omits them, we do not blame him for having neglected a strict duty. Accordingly we do not feel that the person to whom such a duty might or might not be fulfilled has a right that it be performed.

(*c*) Most people would say that we have duties to animals, but some might be chary of saying that animals have rights against us.

(*d*) When a man has a duty to himself, are we to say he has a right against himself?

We must see whether our proposed scheme can deal with these difficulties. Does it clearly discord with common-sense judgements in these four types of instance? Or can it account for them all?

(*a*) I am inclined to deny that there is a strict obligation to realize goodness as such. It does not seem to me that I am morally bound to increase the amount of virtue, or of aesthetic appreciation, in the world, as I am morally bound to help persons in need. Virtue and aesthetic appreciation are good, and to increase the amount of such good existing in the world is right in Moore's sense of 'right', i.e. it is to cause the existence of good. I suggest that when we say it is right to promote the increase of virtue, knowledge, and beauty, we just mean that such action causes good to exist. We approve of such increase. We might say that it is 'morally fitting', but this seems to me a weaker notion than the incumbency of moral obligation.

(*b*) From an objective point of view, the so-called 'duties of supererogation' are not duties. To say that they are supererogatory is to say, in terms, that they go beyond duty. Yet in saying that they are *duties* of supererogation we seem to contradict ourselves. I think the reason why we call them duties is that the agent of such actions may himself think of them as duties. Not always, by any means. Such acts are more often done from good motives (what we have called 'excellences of character') other than the moral motive. But sometimes they may be done from thought of duty. Then for the agent they *are* duties, but from the objective standpoint, i.e. from the standpoint of what we take to be the average moral agent, they are thought to go beyond duty and so are not duties. Correspondingly, in the eyes of the agent the beneficiary has a right, while from the objective standpoint (in the imagined eye of the average impartial spectator) the person benefited does not possess a right. The beneficiary would not be entitled to assert that he has a right, for in asserting a right (that is, in asserting that someone else has a duty to us) we think, and are only entitled to think, of the agent as being an average moral agent and not as being a specially saintly person. The agent himself, however, in thinking that he has a *duty* to the beneficiary to do the act, is *ipso facto* thinking of the beneficiary as having a right to the service in question. No doubt we should not say so in common speech, for we hesitate to assign rights which could not be reasonably claimed by the person himself who is said to have the right, or by someone on his behalf. But if the agent thinks, though the average moral agent would not think, that he has a duty to perform, e.g., a particular act of charity, he must be thinking of the need which the charitable act will relieve as *calling for* the act of charity, and this is just another way of saying that he thinks of the need as constituting a moral claim.

The above account of 'duties of supererogation' seems to

imply that 'thinking makes it so'. I believe this to be in a sense true. Further elucidation must await discussion of the metaphysic of morals.

(*c*) It might be said that so-called duties to animals are not really duties. As with the alleged obligation to realize good, it might be urged, these acts are 'fitting' but not strictly obligatory. Kant[1] seems to have held that duties could only be toward rational beings. This view, however, does not appear to me to accord with experience. If I see an animal or bird in pain, the rightness of relieving the pain if I can is not like the rightness of promoting culture for its intrinsic value. It seems to me to be a moral obligation proper, an action incumbent on me, something that I owe *to* the animal or bird as a sensitive creature. But if I owe the action *to* the creature, that is the same as saying the creature has a claim.

Some theorists find difficulty in attributing claims and rights to animals because animals cannot recognize claims. To the assertion that something cannot exist if not recognized, the obvious answer, in epistemological discussion, is that the existence of a thing cannot depend on recognition; if it is the sort of thing that can be recognized, then it must be there, independent of the recognition, in order to be recognized. The claim of a man does not depend on his recognizing it, and therefore an animal might have a claim although it does not recognize and is incapable of recognizing its claim. A child may be incapable of recognizing his claims, yet they are there. Both with children and with animals, the claim might be recognized by adult rational onlookers, but in any event the existence of the claim does not depend on recognition by anyone. This, as I say, is the stock epistemological reply to the view that rights depend on recognition. As I have already indicated in discussing duties of supererogation, however, it seems to me that the existence of moral characteristics is somehow made by thought. If this is true, the epistemological doctrine that a thing must first exist in order to be recognized,

[1]And Richard Price on second thoughts—see editor's footnote on p. 151 of my edition of the *Review of Morals*.

might not apply to what is denoted by moral concepts. We must discuss later in what respect thought is essential to the existence of moral characteristics. At present, in the logic of morals, I think we can accept the definition of a claim or right as something owed *to* a potential recipient. With this definition in mind, to say that animals have claims and rights is simply another way of saying that men have obligations and duties to animals. It is no doubt true that the ordinary usage of 'claim' contains some thought of the person who has the claim making it, *claiming* his due. To this extent the term 'claim' is perhaps less suitable than some other, if it could be found, that does not bear that connotation. But if we remember that by a 'claim' we intend to mean simply a service owed to a potential recipient, there is no objection to saying that animals have claims and rights. The place of animals in the moral scheme of things, while puzzling and instructive for moral theory, does not raise any valid objection to the particular kind of correlation between duties and rights, obligations and claims, that is maintained in our logic of morals.

The situation of animals would constitute an objection to a scheme which asserted the correlation of duties and rights in a different sense. The doctrine that duties and rights are correlative could be taken to mean that the statement '*A* has a duty to *B*' implies, not (or not merely) '*B* has a right against *A*', but '*A* has a right against *B*'; and correspondingly, that the statement '*B* has a right against *A*' implies '*B* has a duty to *A*'. If we were asserting this kind of correlation, then to say that animals have rights would imply that they also have duties, which is absurd. But our logic does not maintain the correlation of duties and rights in this sense, which indeed applies only to a certain class of obligations, the contractual, where the initial situation really is that *both A and B* voluntarily undertake or accept obligations to each other, each on the understanding that the other does likewise, so that their mutual obligations and claims are all linked up at the start.

(d) I am inclined to say that a man has no strict obligations to himself, that the so-called duties to self are either necessary

means to the fulfilment of duties to others, or else are actions which are means to the realization of good and are therefore approved or thought 'fitting' or 'right' in the weak sense of 'right' in which it means good-producing. Thus we do not *blame* a man for imprudence, though we may at times think he has acted, not merely foolishly, but 'improperly'. When we blame a man for neglecting to improve his character, we are thinking of the effects of this on the probability of his fulfilling his duties to others.

We speak of a right to pursue our own happiness. This means that there is a right of action, i.e. that there is nothing wrong in the pursuit of happiness, which is a summary way of referring to men's wishes for themselves. A right of action implies also a claim (of recipience) to liberty, a claim against other men that they do not interfere with one's pursuit of happiness. That is to say, men have an obligation towards others in regard to the latter's pursuit of happiness. But they have no such obligation towards themselves. Prudence is 'fitting' but not obligatory. The 'superiority', analogous to the 'authority' of conscience, which Butler ascribed to 'cool self-love' is the 'obligation' of the hypothetical imperative. Every man desires his own happiness and will naturally seek it. It is reasonable to expect him to seek it. It would be quite unreasonable, because contrary to the strongest impulses of his nature, to expect him wholly to sacrifice it, though at times it is a duty to sacrifice part of our own happiness for the sake of others. We all seek our own interest, and there is nothing wrong in doing so unless we thereby neglect our duties; but there is no moral obligation to seek it. If a man is imprudent, we call him a fool but not a knave.

It may be argued that the obligatoriness of prudence may be deduced from the fact that we think it justifiable to neglect a small obligation to others if the fulfilment of it would involve great sacrifice of the agent's happiness. We should certainly not blame a man who refused to make the sacrifice. My view (it may be said) suggests that such a man neglects his duty for the sake of something which is not a moral obligation, and that he is therefore worthy of blame. But if a great amount of one's own happiness can outweigh a small obligation to others, the two must be commensurate, and this seems to imply that the pursuit of one's own happiness is obligatory, though perhaps only to a small degree.[1]

I do not think we need admit this. An obligation is something a man *can* do. Our desire for our own happiness being so strong, it is not psychologically possible for most men to make a great sacrifice of their own happiness when faced with the possibility of a small service to others. When we say that service to others is an obligation, we imply that it is so if within the agent's power. But when we find that it involves a great sacrifice of the agent's own welfare, so as to make the action psychologically impossible for most men, we do not think there is any obligation in such circumstances, and we do not blame the agent for failing to do the action. We think him 'justified' in preferring his own happiness, in the sense that he has contravened no obligation, for what at first sight appeared to be an obligation turns out not to have been one. Confirmation of this view is provided if we consider how we should judge an unusually altruistic agent who, in the suggested situation, does make the great sacrifice of his own interest in order to perform a small service to others. We should admire him for having performed a work of supererogation (as it appears to us, though in his eyes it may be required by duty). We might at times call him quixotic, but we should not condemn him as having neglected his true duty. In so far as the adjective 'quixotic' suggests a faint whiff of condemnation, I suspect that this is because we think such a man might, when faced in other circumstances with conflicting obligations, be carried away by impulsive generosity or give too great weight to the obligatoriness of a possible act of immediate beneficence in comparison with other obligations. I do not think the adjective involves any moral condemnation of his present action. It does carry the suggestion that he is foolish, but we have agreed that imprudence is folly.

[1]Cf. Carritt, *Ethical and Political Thinking*, p. 114.

I should say, then, that the seeking of one's own happiness is not itself a moral obligation. But it is 'fitting', for it is a means to good. It may be indirectly obligatory as a necessary means to the fulfilment of our duties. The virtues of self-improvement are more obviously a necessary means to the maximum fulfilment of duty, and they are also in themselves 'fitting' as being the realization of good.

From this discussion I conclude that the relations between duties and rights, obligations and claims, that are involved in our logic of moral concepts can stand. But in the course of answering the objection raised by the above four types of obligation or alleged obligation, I have more than once referred to the notion of 'moral fittingness' or propriety as something different from moral obligation. How does this new concept fit into our logic of morals?

§4. *Fittingness*

Dr. A. C. Ewing has attempted to use the idea of fittingness as the sole ultimate ethical notion, i.e. to construct a logic of moral concepts based on a single ethical term. In his book, *The Definition of Good,*[1] Dr. Ewing says he is defining 'good' in terms of 'ought'. This suggests that his scheme would represent a simplification of our provisionally accepted logic of moral concepts, in which 'ought' and 'good' are the two basic concepts. The simplification would be in the reverse direction to that taken by the pure agathism of Moore's *Principia Ethica;* Dr. Ewing defines 'good' in terms of 'ought', while Professor Moore defined 'ought' in terms of 'good'. In fact, however, the 'ought' that Dr. Ewing uses as his basic concept is not the 'ought' of obligation, which formed one of our two basic concepts. His use of 'ought' is equivalent to the weaker notion of 'fitting', and his suggestion is that *both* of our basic concepts, goodness and obligation, can be analysed in terms of this third concept, fittingness.

Dr. Ewing defines 'good' as 'what ought to be the object of

[1]Ch. v.

a pro attitude'[1] or as the 'fitting object of a pro attitude'.[2] ' "Pro attitude" is intended to cover any favourable attitude to something. It covers, for instance, choice, desire, liking, pursuit, approval, admiration.'[3] His suggestion is that 'good' can be defined in terms of the ethical notion 'ought' and the non-ethical, but descriptively psychological, notion of favourable attitudes. He takes care to point out that the 'ought' which he employs in his definition of 'good' is not the 'ought' of obligation but the 'ought' of fittingness.

Dr. Ewing proceeds later to give a tentative analysis of obligation in terms of fittingness, regarding the former as a more complex notion. He suggests that '*A* is obliged to do this' means:

(1) It would be fitting for *A* to do this, and

(2) If he does not do this, it is fitting that he should be in that respect an object of the emotion of moral disapproval (i.e., if he does not do it, he deserves blame).[4]

Dr. Ewing is not sure that this exhausts the whole meaning of obligation. He suggests that when a person is conscious of a duty he has three thoughts in mind. The first and second of these are the two propositions included in Dr. Ewing's definition of moral obligation. The third element is 'the concept that there is in some sense a law binding him to do it, which law, while it does not compel in the sense of taking away his liberty to disobey it, yet has authority in another meaning of the term, so that morality consists in acting as if he were compelled by it'.[5] Dr. Ewing suggests that the third element may be, or may involve, a theological concept. But he recognizes that his definition of obligation may be unsatisfactory in failing to do justice to the third element, and in that case, he allows, we shall have to admit two indefinable concepts in ethics, fittingness and moral obligation.

The whole question at issue here turns on the third element, which does not find a place in Dr. Ewing's definition in terms of fittingness. I should have thought that this third ele-

[1] p. 148. [2] p. 152. [3] p. 149. [4] pp. 168-9. [5] pp. 170-1.

ment gave the essential meaning of moral obligation, while the two propositions that form Dr. Ewing's definition are concerned, at best, with peripheral implications of the idea of moral obligation. Is this third element a theological or a moral concept? Kant's moral philosophy, which emphasizes more than any other the idea of moral law, gives an account of its bindingness which is not theological, and Dr. Ewing is himself hesitant in his suggestion that theology is involved. My own view of the presuppositions of moral obligation will come out in my discussion of the metaphysic of morals. In the logic of morals it must suffice to say that, as Dr. Ewing himself is partially inclined to think, analysis of obligation in terms of fittingness does not bring out the essential meaning, which is bindingness on the agent. This is a stronger notion than fittingness, and a different notion, for it refers primarily to the agent while fittingness refers primarily to the act. To define obligation in terms of the fittingness of acts to situations is no more satisfactory than Professor Moore's definition in terms of good results. For the notion of obligation expresses incumbency on a man. It is *he* that is obliged. If we speak simply of the characteristics of a situation and the relation of a possible act to that situation,—if we say that the consequential situation would be good or that the act would be fitting to the existing situation, the agent may still ask, What's fittingness to him, or he to fittingness? Unless the fittingness or the goodness is linked to him by the notion of obligation, of *his* being obliged or required to act, he may shrug his shoulders. Again, the goodness or fittingness is not something that now exists but a characteristic that would exist if he did the act, while his obligation exists now before he acts; it is an obligation *to* act. Should we remove this particular objection by saying that his present thought of what would be good or fitting is the ground of his present obligation, this only brings into greater relief the fact that obligation is not the same notion as fittingness. We must postulate the *synthetic* principle that a man is obliged to do what he thinks is fitting.

Nor is a statement of obligation equivalent to a statement

of the appropriate reaction by others to the agent's omission to act. It is a categorical, positive statement about the agent now, not a statement about spectators in the future event of a negative hypothesis concerning the agent being fulfilled. I conclude that obligation can no more be defined in terms of fittingness than of good, and therefore I retain it as a primitive concept in our logic of morals.

What of Dr. Ewing's more assured contention, that 'good' may be defined in terms of fittingness? Our consideration of certain types of right action that are not strictly obligatory led us to include the notion of fittingness in our logic. If we can now discard 'good' as being an amalgam of 'fitting' with certain non-ethical terms, that will mean two basic concepts instead of three. We began with two, 'ought' and 'good', but seemed obliged to add a third, 'fitting'. If we can make 'fitting' a basic concept, and 'good' a derivative one from that, we return to the relative simplicity of two primitive notions.

The proposed reduction seems commendable on other grounds also. For the idea of intrinsic, non-natural good as something wider than, or different from, virtue or moral good, has had very little place in the ethical theory of modern Europe. (Plato of course talks of absolute good, but his is a notion very akin to beauty, and further, his description of it as absolute depends more on his theory of universals generally than on considerations applying specifically to ethics. For Aristotle, the idea of good is at any rate not divorced from psychological attitudes.) In the British tradition of moral philosophy, those theorists who have concentrated on the idea of good have been (until Moore) naturalists, while the non-naturalists have concentrated on obligation or rightness and have had little or nothing to say of intrinsic, non-natural good other than moral good, while yet introducing at times the concept of fittingness. Again, when Moore defined 'right' as the cause of a good result, this had some plausibility because one sense of 'right' (in which it means the same as 'fitting') does seem to be interchangeable with 'realizing good'. Sometimes when we say that an act, e.g. of supererogation, is right, we can express the same idea by saying that it is worthy or good, or else a means to good.

A further advantage of analysing 'good' in terms of 'fitting' is, as Dr. Ewing points out,[1] that it gets rid of the separate notion of evil. A thing we call evil will be the fitting object of an unfavourable attitude. To adopt fittingness in place of good and evil as a basic concept therefore means greater simplicity. It also brings out a parallelism with our other basic concept, for the idea of obligation has no contrary. The adjective 'wrong' is the contrary of the adjective 'right', but translated in terms of obligation a wrong act is one from which the agent is positively obliged to refrain. There are obligations to act and obligations to refrain from proposed actions, just as there are acts and situations toward which it is fitting to take a favourable attitude and others toward which it is fitting to take an unfavourable attitude. An indifferent act is one in regard to which there is no obligation either to proceed or to refrain, and in regard to which neither a favourable attitude nor an unfavourable attitude is fitting.

In our logic of moral concepts, therefore, we shall replace the concept of good by that of fittingness, and we shall follow Dr. Ewing in defining 'good' and 'bad' in terms of it. 'X is good' is defined as 'X is a fitting object of a favourable attitude' (including pursuit, the word 'attitude' being loosely used, as by Ewing, to include certain types of action). 'X is bad' is defined as 'X is a fitting object of an unfavourable attitude' (including prevention and removal). Hence to say that the consequences of an act would be good is to imply analytically that it is fitting to try to realize those consequences by doing the act, but it does not imply that there is an obligation to do so. Our logic allows that 'X is good' implies 'The pursuit of X is right' in the weaker sense of 'right', that it is, if you like, a 'duty' of imperfect obligation, but in our logic that is not strictly a duty at all. Likewise, 'X is bad' implies that the prevention of X (if not already in existence) or the removal of X (if already existing) is fitting.

[1]pp. 167-8.

We accordingly translate the so-called duties of imperfect obligation in terms of fittingness, and thereby reach logical equivalence (mutual implication) between the rightness of such acts and the goodness which those acts realize. We thereby do justice to the force of agathism, and indeed strengthen its position by making the implications involved analytic, as Moore tried to do. At the same time, however, we do justice to the difficulties brought against agathism by deontology, and to the universal feeling that there is a difference of kind between the so-called duties of perfect obligation and duties of imperfect obligation.

We are using 'obligation' only where there is a correlative claim. This seems to me in accordance with the connotation of strict obligation, which refers to a tie to others, an owing of something to them, to which they accordingly have a claim. 'Obligation' and 'claim' analytically imply each other, as do 'fitting' and 'good'. We are calling an obligation a duty if it is the only obligation, or the one judged strongest, occurring in the situation. The correlative of a duty we are calling a right. Hence the following implications hold good. The proposition 'X is a duty (or a right)' analytically implies 'X is an obligation (or a claim)'. The proposition 'X is an obligation (or a claim)', *together with* the proposition 'No other obligations (or claims) now confront the agent' *or with* the proposition 'All other obligations (or claims) now confronting the agent are judged weaker than X', analytically imply the proposition 'X is a duty (or a right)'.

In our logic, there are two sets of terms, (1) obligations, duties, claims, rights, and (2) fittingness and good. Each of the two has a high degree of internal coherence, but is logically independent of the other set. Is there, then, no relationship between the two sets of terms? I think there is. Fittingness is, in certain circumstances, a sort of half-way house to obligation. But this relationship is a matter to be dealt with in the metaphysic of morals, where the presuppositions of the two will be brought out. In our logic of morals they have different meanings and are independent of each other.

V

JUSTICE

The claims of justice present special problems both for our logic of moral concepts and for the logic of moral principles. (1) We left aside earlier the notion of desert, and we must consider whether this is, or involves, a basic ethical concept additional to those we have already allowed or whether it may be analysed by reference to them. Utilitarians have commonly regarded the ethical content of desert or merit as residing in the goodness of the results of the treatment described as 'deserved', while deontologists have opposed this view. (2) A second problem arises when it is claimed by some, and denied by others, that justice demands equality in some sense. The idea of equality is not itself a moral concept. What is disputed here is whether there is a moral principle to the effect that all men ought to be treated equally.

§1. *Classification of the claims of justice*

Justice has been traditionally divided into three species, (*a*) distributive justice, (*b*) retributive or corrective justice, (*c*) commutative justice. I take (*a*) to refer to a principle of equality in some sense, and (*b*) to refer to the claims of reparation and of desert; (c) is the claim that contracts be fair. The three together make up the idea of equity or fairness, a frequent constituent of moral judgements, which I regard as synonymous with justice. In law, the word 'justice' is used in a wide sense to cover all legal procedure and decisions, while the word 'equity', in English Law at least, is used, for historical reasons, to cover one part of legal justice, the part originally issuing from the Court of Chancery, which then developed into the Courts of Equity. (These are now incorporated in the comprehensive High Court of Justice, which uses both the rules of Common Law and the rules of Equity.)

Here, however, I use both the word 'justice' and the word 'equity' (or 'fairness') in the common, non-legal acceptation, in which they are roughly synonymous, while forming only a part of the requirements of morality. In this acceptation, 'justice' or 'equity' is commonly opposed to beneficence or utility. By giving an account of justice, then, we shall *ipso facto* be giving an account of the concept of fairness or equity. It is true that the threefold classification of the elements of justice given above seems to omit one notion that is involved in the idea of equity, that of making special provision for special need. We say that it is 'only fair' to make special provision for the handicapped, e.g. the disabled or feeble-minded, or for those who have fallen on evil days through the accidents of fortune such as poverty or sickness. I shall suggest, however, that the claim of special provision for special need is simply a consequence of the equality principle, the claim of distributive justice.

The difficulty in the case of (*a*), distributive justice, is to be sure what sort of equality is felt to be properly claimed. Equality of what? Of consideration, and if so what does that involve? Of opportunity? Of material goods? Or of happiness? This difficulty we shall consider shortly. For the moment we shall simply note that none of the possible answers to the question raised contains a constituent which is an ethical term, so that the problem involved in the claim to equality does not concern the logic of moral concepts. The notion of equality itself is likewise not an ethical concept. The ethical content enters in the *claim* to equality, in the demand that each man *ought* to receive equality of whatever we decide the material content of the claim to be. The ethical term involved is that of 'claim' or 'ought to receive'. The relation of this to the 'ought' of obligation we have already considered in Chapter IV. To say that a man has a claim to, or 'ought' to receive, some benefit, is simply another way of saying that some other person or group of persons ought to give him that benefit.

I shall take next species (*c*), commutative justice. This provides relatively little difficulty for the logic of morals. It states that in contractual dealings between man and man, the bargain struck ought to be fair and ought to be kept. To say that a contract or a promise ought to be kept, is simply to bring out the fact that the making of a contract or a promise is laying oneself under an obligation to do what one undertakes to do. To say that the bargain struck in a contract ought to be fair, means that the benefits exchanged should be judged or acknowledged to be of roughly equal value. A bargain is unfair if one of the participants has, without the knowledge or against the will of the other, secured an advantage greater than that which the other receives. The content of the claim to mutual equality here does not give rise to any special philosophical difficulty, although in practice there may be great difficulty in deciding how to compare the respective values of quite different things. Nor is the 'value', which has to be equal on both sides, an ethical notion; it is rather an economic one, and is to be analysed in naturalistic terms. As to the moral 'claims' of the parties concerned, these are again analytically correlative to their obligations to each other. But in the case of contracts, the obligations and claims involved are doubly correlative; *A*'s claim against *B* implies not only (1) that *B* has an obligation to *A*, but also (2) that *A* has an obligation to *B* (corresponding to *B*'s claim against *A*). As was pointed out in Chapter IV, §3, the second kind of correlation between obligations and claims arises in the case of contracts simply because a contract is at the start a mutual undertaking of obligations to each other by both parties. Each takes upon himself his obligation on condition that the other undertakes an equivalent obligation to him. Thus the obligation which each incurs is a conditional one, involving the incurrence of a like obligation by the other party. Being of this conditional and mutually involving nature, the obligations of contract analytically imply each other, as well as analytically implying, like all obligations, a claim in the party to whom the obligation is incurred. Contracts, like the one-sided undertaking of an obligation that we call a promise, present a philosophical difficulty in that they seem to be the creation of obligations by the mere utterance of words. This, however, is a metaphysical, not a logical, difficulty. No new ethical terms are involved. To make a promise or a contract is deliberately to take upon oneself an obligation. The only ethical terms involved are those of obligation and claim.

We come finally to species (*b*), retributive or corrective justice. This covers the claims of reparation and of desert. (1) The word 'reparation' here is used in a wider sense than the normal, to mean both the making good of injury (the ordinary sense of 'reparation') and the readiness to requite benefits that is implied in the obligation of gratitude; both include the making of equal return, in the one case for loss that the person now obliged has caused, in the other for benefit that he has received. Here again, no new ethical term is involved. We think that a man who has received a benefit, or who has (wittingly or unwittingly) deprived another of some satisfaction, ought to be prepared to make up by conferring equivalent benefit if required. The ethical term involved is, as in distributive and commutative justice, that of obligation. (2) With the requital of desert, however, a further ethical term is involved, and we must consider how this is to be fitted into our logic of moral concepts. 'Desert' refers primarily to the merit of virtue and the demerit of vice, in consequence of which the first is thought to call for reward and the second for punishment. The ideas of 'merit' and 'reward' are also extended to express the praise accorded to certain non-moral capacities and activities and to the benefits that are accordingly regarded as their due.

Theorists who deny or ignore the alleged claim to equality sometimes treat the claim of desert, i.e. the apportionment of happiness or the means to it in accordance with merit (or perhaps merit and capacity), as *distributive* justice, since such apportionment is, in their view, the one proper principle of distribution. Sir David Ross,[1] for example, uses the word 'justice' to refer to the distribution of happiness in accordance with desert, and evidently does not recognize any claim to

[1] *The Right and the Good*, pp. 21, 26-7, 138.

equality other than the 'proportionate equality' which Aristotle declares such distribution to be. The word 'retribution' may then be used to refer solely to one way, not necessarily the right way, of looking at punishment. Since I shall argue that there is, in the moral thinking of our society at least, a claim to equality other than the so-called 'proportionate equality', I retain the name of distributive justice for the claim to equality, and I subsume the requital of desert, whether by way of reward or by way of punishment, under retributive justice.[1] If this diversity of usage is confusing, we may talk simply of the alleged principle or claim of equality and the alleged principle or claim of desert.

I have spoken, for the moment, of *alleged* principles of equality and desert, because it may be denied that either of them is a moral principle standing on its own. As we have seen, it may be denied that there is any valid claim to equality, except where distribution according to desert requires, as a special case, equal distribution to those of equal desert. Deontologists generally agree that the principle of desert is a cardinal, if not the sole, element in justice and that this is different from, and may conflict with, considerations of social utility. Some of them, for example Richard Price and Sir David Ross, do not recognize as an additional element of justice any claim to equality. Conversely, the hedonistic utilitarians regarded the idea of desert as falling under the claim of utility, while (in their unconfused thought) they felt bound to posit a principle of equality separate from the obligation to promote general happiness as such. Bentham and Mill seem to have supposed at times that their principle of 'counting everyone for one' followed, like the principle of requiting desert, from the principle of utility, that '*ipsa utilitas*' was wholly '*iusti mater et aequi*'. But the clearest thinker of the utilitarian persuasion, Sidgwick, recognized explicitly that such considerations as 'counting everyone for one' (which he called principles of 'equity') were separate from the principle of producing as much happiness as possible.

[1]Cf. Carritt, *Ethical and Political Thinking*, ch. ix.

I propose to consider first, whether the concept of desert can be analysed in terms of other concepts, and in particular whether it can be reduced to that of social utility. I shall argue that the utilitarian analysis is inadequate. Nevertheless, I shall suggest that the idea of desert does not need to be added as a further basic notion to our logic of moral concepts, but can be analysed by reference to the ideas of obligation and claim. I shall next consider whether there is a positive claim to equality, and if so, in what sense. Although the claims of desert and equality need separate treatment, my conclusions will suggest that the reason why they are both subsumed under the one concept of justice is that both represent protections of the interests of the individual, and as such, they are, I shall argue, not fundamentally different from the thought that is basic to the idea of liberty. The nineteenth-century utilitarians emphasized the liberty of the individual in their political and economic theories, but their theory of ethics seems to me to neglect the importance of the individual, and this is brought out by an examination of the idea of justice, which forms the greatest stumbling-block to the acceptance of utilitarianism.

§2. *Desert*

We say that virtue merits reward and vice punishment. Or again we say that happiness ought to be proportioned to desert. How is this idea of desert or merit to be fitted into our logic of moral concepts? Can we analyse it in terms of some moral concept already admitted to the system?

Can we say that the notion of desert may be analysed in terms of 'ought'? That '*A* deserves happiness' is equivalent to '*A* ought to be happy', and that '*B* deserves pain' is equivalent to '*B* ought to be pained'? If we say this, we are using 'ought', not in the sense of obligation, 'ought to do', but in the sense of claim, 'ought to receive'. It seems odd to say that a guilty person has a *claim* to be pained, just as it seems odd to say that animals have claims, because we cannot imagine the supposed possessors of these claims *claiming* their due. But in our logic, to say that a potential recipient has a claim is the same as saying that a potential agent ought to give him that to which he is said to have a claim. So that the 'claim' language would be permissible if we agreed that '*A* deserves *X*' means 'Someone ought to give *X* to *A*'.

Do we, however, always think this? That wherever a man is deserving of good or ill, someone ought to give him his deserts? Difficulty arises with ill-desert. If a man has deliberately done wrong when he could have done right, we say he deserves punishment, but does this mean or imply in every case that someone ought to punish him? The trend of modern opinion is that the actual infliction of punishment is to be justified only if it will lead to a balance of good, that it is to be justified by utilitarian considerations of deterrence and reform. Where there is an obligation to punish, therefore, the obligation seems to depend, at least in part, on the future consequences of the act. But desert clearly depends not on the future but on the past. The statement that a man deserves punishment is justified by the fact that he *has* deliberately acted contrary to duty. To say that he deserves punishment, then, cannot mean the same as saying that someone ought to punish him, for the two statements differ in their implications. The first implies that he has acted contrary to duty, and implies nothing about future consequences. The second implies that the punishment will have good consequences, though it also implies that the man deserves to be punished. The second includes the first but also goes beyond it.

Utilitarians attempt to cut this knot in the following way. They hold that punishment is justified solely by its consequences. The idea of ill-desert, included in that of punishment, is a concealed way of referring to, and achieving, good consequences. According to the utilitarian account of punishment, '*A* deserves punishment' means: (1) '*A* has done an act of a type that is harmful to the public and that tends to be prevented by punishment or the threat of it.' (2) 'Therefore, it will be useful to punish him.' The word 'punishment' here simply means the infliction of pain, with the promise of its repetition, in circumstances where a socially harmful tendency manifests itself and is of such a nature that fear of pain can cause the suppression or inhibition of future manifestations. When we say that the punishment 'fits' the crime, we are referring, not to any specifically ethical relation between them, but simply to the causal property which the punishment has of tending to remove or repress the harmful tendency. A similar account, *mutatis mutandis,* would be given of meriting reward. (A forceful modern statement of this theory of punishment and reward is to be found in Mr. P. Nowell-Smith's article, 'Freewill and Moral Responsibility', published in *Mind,* January, 1948.)

The objections to this account are twofold. (1) Punishment and reward are not the sole type of action (or indeed of painful and pleasurable action) that is useful in averting public harm or promoting public good. Quarantine is useful in averting public harm, and it happens to involve, as imprisonment designedly includes, the experience of isolation, which to most people is unpleasant. Instruction makes people useful to society, and to some it is pleasant (and so like reward), to others painful (and so like punishment). Taking medicine benefits society as well as the patient, since a sick person is a burden on society; and it may be unpleasant. Yet it is not called punishment. Sermons are intended to strengthen our morality, to reinforce our virtue and to correct our vice; the virtuous may perhaps find them gratifying, and the vicious may find them tedious. Are we to say that sermons are rewards to the one and punishments to the other? These are the stock criticisms of the simpler utilitarian theories of punishment, that they would assimilate to punishment all prevention of social harm and all reform. The more elaborate utilitarian theory outlined above would avoid calling some (though not all) of our examples by the name of punishment, since it recognizes that punishment differs from other types of deterrence and reform in looking to guilt and consequent ill-desert. But it gives a secondary utilitarian account of 'guilt' and 'desert', which is open to a similar sort of criticism, namely that it is too wide. This defect of the utilitarian analysis of desert constitutes our second objection.

(2) On the utilitarian theory of desert, we should have to say, where any action causes the removal of an undesirable tendency or the strengthening of a desirable one, not only that the action is to be called punishment or reward, but that the person to whom it is directed 'deserves' it, since the 'propriety' or 'fittingness' of desert simply expresses this causal relation, in the same sense in which medicine is 'appropriate' for the cure of sickness. Indeed, the sick person 'deserves' his medicine. The donkey deserves his blows or carrots, and his laziness or energy are to be called immoral or moral. We do not in fact use the language of morality in such circumstances. When we speak of desert we imply that the agent knew what he was doing, could control his action at that time, and was aware of a right and a wrong. We say that punishment is justified when it is *both* useful *and* deserved.

So far we have reached the following negative conclusions. '*A* deserves punishment' is not equivalent to 'Someone ought to punish *A*' nor to 'The punishing of *A* will be useful'. The expression implies that *A* has deliberately done wrong, but this is not the whole of its meaning, for the notion we are concerned to analyse, desert, is regarded as a connecting link between the past state of affairs and the receipt of pain.

I agree with the utilitarian theory of punishment to the extent of thinking that where there is an obligation to punish, the obligation arises from utility. The strength of the so-called retributive (or, as I prefer to call it, the desert) theory of punishment lies, not in the justification of a positive obligation to punish the guilty, but in the protection of innocence. The utilitarian theory, taken alone, requires us to say, with Samuel Butler's Erewhonians, that sickness is a crime which deserves the punishment of medicine. It also requires us to say, when 'it is expedient that one man should die for the people', that he deserves this as a punishment. It is here that common sense protests against the 'injustice' of utilitarianism, and it is here that the 'retributive' theory of punishment has greatest force.

Punishment is permissible only if it is deserved. But this does not of itself give rise to an obligation to punish. An obligation to inflict punishment, where punishment is permitted by desert, arises from the social utility of its infliction. The desert permits this socially useful action to be taken although it means pain to the particular person concerned. Where there is no guilt, the infliction of pain on a particular person may still be socially useful, but the claim of social utility is opposed by the claim of the individual to be treated as an 'end-in-himself' and not merely as a means to the ends of society. Where, however, a person is guilty of having wilfully done wrong, he has thereby forfeited part of his claim to be treated as an end-in-himself; in acting as a non-moral being he leaves it open to his fellows to use him as such.[1] Such forfeit of his claim not to be pained does not of itself give rise to an obligation to pain him, for his ill-desert consists in the removal, not the creation, of a claim with its corresponding obligation. The guilt does not constitute, or give rise to, a claim on the part of the guilty person to be punished, i.e. an obligation on the part of others to punish him. It removes, to the degree to which he has infringed another's rights, his normal claim not to be pained; i.e., it removes, to that degree, the obligation of others not to pain him. Where there is a positive obligation to punish him, this is the obligation to the public at large to safeguard their security, and the corresponding claim is the claim of the public to have their security safeguarded.

This obligation to, or claim of, the public at large, exists of course at all times, and if the fulfilment of it involves pain for an innocent individual it still has its force. But the claim of the public in such circumstances conflicts with the claim of the individual not to be pained, to be treated as an end, and sometimes the one claim, sometimes the other, is thought to be paramount in the circumstances. If it should be thought necessary to override the claim of the individual for the sake of the claim of society, our decision is coloured by compunction,

[1]Cf. W. G. Maclagan, 'Punishment and Retribution' (*Philosophy*, July, 1939), section v.

which we express by saying that the claim of justice has to give way to that of utility. Where the individual has been guilty of deliberate wrongdoing, however, his claim not to be pained is thought to be removed; there is held to be no conflict of claims now, no moral *obstat*[1] raised by justice to the fulfilment of the claim of utility. This thought is expressed by saying that the individual 'deserves' his pain, and the pain is called 'punishment', which is simply a way of saying that in this situation the infliction of pain, for the sake of social utility, involves no trespass on the claims of justice, no conflict between utility and justice. What is called 'punishment' is not a different sort of *fact* from any other pain inflicted for utilitarian purposes; it receives a different *name* to express the thought that the pain is inflicted in circumstances where it commits no offence against justice. Justice is 'satisfied' by the 'punishment', for justice has not, in the circumstances of guilt, a countervailing claim that would have been breached by pursuing the path of utility.

In giving this interpretation of the saying that 'justice is satisfied by punishment', I do not imply that the statement has always had the meaning which I am now attributing to it (or rather, recommending for it). Clearly it used to have a more positive meaning. No doubt it originally referred to the satisfaction of the desire for vengeance. My point is that our present moral thinking recoils, as opponents of the retributive theory rightly insist, from justifying punishment by mere retaliation, but at the same time it does give an important place to justice in the idea of punishment. This rôle of justice, I am suggesting, is the protection of innocence, the raising of a moral *obstat* to the infliction of pain on an innocent individual. Where we think that, despite the moral *obstat* of justice, the pain must be inflicted for the sake of utility, we recognize the claim of justice at least to the extent of using

[1]There is always the weaker *obstat* of unfittingness in the infliction of pain. My point is that the *obstat* of a moral claim is not only greater in degree but also different in kind, and the difference of kind is marked by the use of different language.

different language. It may be *expedient,* but not just, that one man should die for the people. 'Expediency' then has the a-moral or anti-moral connotation which it bears when 'expediency' is contrasted with 'principle'. But where the victim of expediency is guilty, he has forfeited the claim of justice; now we may speak of his pain as 'punishment', as 'deserved'. Expediency here does not conflict with 'principle', i.e. with justice, but conforms to 'principle'. Not that the punishment is now *required* by justice. The 'principle' that requires the 'punishment' is the principle of safeguarding public security, i.e. expediency itself. Justice does not demand the punishment; justice stands aside, for it is satisfied that its claims raise no obstruction. It does demand *reparation,* where possible, for the person wronged, and thereby lays an obligation on the wrongdoer toward the person he has wronged. But it lays no obligation on others to *punish* the wrongdoer. It permits the punishment by withdrawing its protection against the claims of expediency. The obligation to punish comes from expediency.

Of course, expediency does not become 'principle' only when justice stands aside. The claim of social utility is always a valid claim. It is the claim of the members of society in general not to be harmed. In denying earlier (in Chapter IV, §3) that there is a moral obligation to produce good as such, I was not denying the partial truth of hedonistic utilitarianism. There is an obligation to relieve and to prevent pain in others. When I say that the utility of punishment gives rise to an obligation, the obligation is to the members of society who will thereby be protected from harm.

By contrasting the claim of justice, as looking to the interests of the individual, with the claim of utility, as looking to the interests of society at large, I do not imply that society is anything other than its members. In our practical deliberations, however, we often find it convenient to think of 'the interests of society' as an abstracted entity, since we may know from experience that a course of action is likely to benefit or harm a number of members of our society, while not knowing which particular members will be affected on this occasion. The dangers of the abstraction are countered by the concept of justice, which emphasizes the claims of the individual as such.

In my suggestion that guilt or ill-desert involves forfeiture of the claim to be treated as an end, I am indebted to Professor W. G. Maclagan's discussion of 'Punishment and Retribution', a paper published in *Philosophy*, July, 1939. Professor Maclagan's view, however, contains two features which I am unable to accept. (1) He holds that although the guilty person forfeits his claim, other persons are, as moral agents, no less obliged than before to treat him as an end. I have said that justice permits but does not require punishment. It may be asked whether this implies that punishment is not wrong even when utility does not provide a positive obligation to punish. My view would be that, where utility does not require punishment, to pain a guilty person is wrong in the sense of 'improper' or 'unfitting' but not in the sense of contravening an obligation. Professor Maclagan seems inclined to think of 'the moral agent' as the ideal moral agent, one to whom, for instance, acts of supererogation would appear as genuine duties. To such a person, acts generally regarded as merely fitting are obligatory;[1] for him, the sphere of obligation covers the whole of the moral life. That such an attitude is the ideal for an individual in his personal relationships, need not be denied. The concept of punishment, however, has no place at all in the personal relationships of a moral individual. The infliction of punishment is a matter for the state, not the individual. The state, as representing the social body, has to deal with men as they are, and to act from the standpoint of the average, and not the ideal, moral agent. The state exists to safeguard the claims of its citizens, and its obligation to punish the guilty is an obligation to protect the citizens who might be harmed by the guilty. It is permitted to pain the guilty for this purpose, because the guilty have forfeited part of *their* claim on the state or social body, i.e., because the state or social body has a diminished obligation to them.

[1]Cf. ch. iv, §3, above.

(2) I am also unable to agree with Professor Maclagan's view that there are no degrees of guilt or of just penalty, that *any* moral failure involves, from the standpoint of the guilty person, *entire* loss of the claim to be treated as an end. Professor Maclagan's reason for this doctrine is that it is impossible, even in principle, to assign degrees to guilt, i.e. to moral failure. I should hold that the degree of a person's guilt, to be equated with the degree of penalty permissible, lies in the degree to which he has infringed another person's rights. A man's duties, on my view, are equivalent to the rights of others against him, so that to infringe a duty is *ipso facto* to infringe a right. It may be (though I should hesitate to admit even this) that the moral nature of the agent is breached just as much by one example of moral failure as by another. But not his status under justice. So far as concerns his relation to the person whom he wrongs, theft is not as heinous as murder. Guilt under justice has degrees, and the degree of punishment deserved depends on what has been done to others.

This is why the ancient Mosaic law, formulating one of the principles of justice, says 'An eye for an eye, a tooth for a tooth'. A man who has knocked out another's tooth does not deserve so great a penalty as one who has knocked out an eye. If he has knocked out a tooth, his desert is to suffer equally, but not more. This does not imply that he should necessarily be punished to the extent of his desert. The Mosaic law was not interpreted by the Hebrew legislators to mean that the wrongdoer should lose his tooth. It was interpreted to mean that he should make good the victim's loss by way of compensation, not that he should suffer the same evil as he had inflicted. This so-called *lex talionis* was concerned with reparation rather than punishment. It represents a claim of justice for the individual who has been wronged. But it also expresses a measure of protection by justice even for the wrongdoer. Natural feelings of revenge would prompt a victim or his sympathizers to hit back harder. The *lex talionis*, far from being a reflection of vengeance, insists that the wrongdoer's forfeit of the usual claim to be treated as an end is limited by the extent of the harm he has caused. No guilty person forfeits the whole of his innocence, and justice protects the innocence that remains.

The idea of demerit, I have suggested, signifies the partial removal of a claim normally present. The idea of merit, of virtue deserving happiness, signifies the presence of an additional claim to those normally present. To say that virtue itself implies a claim to happiness (i.e. an obligation on the part of others to bestow happiness) does not give rise to the same difficulty as saying that vice itself implies an obligation on the part of others to punish it. A virtuous man would of course not claim any reward for his virtue, so that here, as in the case of animals, it seems odd to talk of there being a claim; but all we mean by this is that others have an obligation. When I say that the virtuous man has an additional claim by reason of his virtue, all I mean is that others have an additional obligation to him. The bestowal of further positive happiness upon a person already reasonably content (as opposed to the removal, or the non-infliction, of misery) is, in the general relations between man and man, usually thought to go beyond the requirements of strict obligation, to be the part of a supererogatory beneficence. But if a man has exhibited virtue, we feel (as also in certain situations of special relationship, e.g., between husband and wife, or parent and child) that the addition of further positive happiness is 'called for', that it comes within the sphere of our obligation. Good-desert, then, expresses the presence of an additional claim to the normal (i.e. the existence of an additional obligation on the part of other people toward the virtuous person said to be meritorious), while ill-desert expresses the absence of a normal claim (i.e. the removal of a normal obligation of others toward the person said to exhibit demerit).

The obligation to reward virtue for its own sake is, however, not a strong one, if only because any thought on the part of the virtuous agent that his virtue merits reward is liable to make his motive to some degree interested and to that extent less virtuous. Rewards are usually conferred for the sake of utility, and the utilitarian account of reward covers even more of the truth than does its account of punishment. With punishment, the utilitarian account is deficient in failing to cover the protection of innocence, the claim of which often conflicts with and overrides that of public utility. The claim of virtue, however, usually coincides with that of utility, since the encouragement of virtue is socially useful, and therefore little compunction is felt in accepting the utilitarian justification of reward. If, in some exceptional cases, there is a conflict between the claim of virtue to reward and the claim of public utility, no-one would deny that the claim of utility takes precedence. However, though the non-utilitarian claim of merit is slight, it is there, and when we say that reward should be given not only *pour encourager les autres* but also because it is deserved, the use of the term 'desert' or 'merit' expresses the existence of an additional claim to the normal.

Our conclusion, then, is that the concept of desert involves no additional ethical term to those we have already accepted. It is a way of speaking of the presence or absence of an obligation and claim in special circumstances. Merit asserts the presence of a special obligation and claim, demerit asserts the absence, in the special circumstances, of a normal obligation and claim.

§3. *Desert and liberty*

The main force of retributive justice lies in its assertion of the claim of the innocent individual to be treated as an end and not merely as a means to the general interest. Now when a man is said to have a right (in my language, a claim) to liberty, this means that other men are obliged not to interfere with his legitimate desires. The claim to liberty is the demand for moral protection of the individual's wishes provided these be not themselves contrary to any moral injunction. The claim of retributive justice that the individual who has not 'deserved ill' (i.e., who has not forfeited the protection of justice by wilful wrongdoing) be treated as an end, and his claim to liberty, are two aspects of a single moral claim. They are alternative ways of expressing the same moral demand, that an individual who has not deliberately contravened the requirements of morality be treated as an 'end-in-himself', with the stress on the negative element of not treating him as a means to the ends of others; the demand is that we leave him to pursue his natural ends and do not interfere by going against his desires. The claim of good-desert also requires the person concerned to be treated as an 'end', but with the stress on the positive obligation to 'make his ends our own', which I take to mean that we should seek to obtain for him the happiness that everyone naturally desires. This is of course different from the negative claim of liberty to be left alone.

So far, I have discussed the notion of desert as meaning *morally* deserving. We do, however, also use the concept of desert in a different way. We say that 'enterprise should receive its just reward', that 'genius deserves recognition', that 'the incompetent deserve to fail'. This sense of desert is made up of two notions; first, that certain capacities and activities are socially useful while other activities are socially harmful, and that the encouragement of the former and disparagement of the latter are socially useful; secondly, it also includes the idea that a man has a 'right' to reap the benefits or ill effects of his own activities. The latter idea suggests that a man has a 'right' to, or 'deserves', the natural consequences of the exercise of capacities or defects for the possession of which he is not *morally* deserving of praise or blame. I do not think it plays so important a part in our idea of non-moral desert as does the idea of social utility, but it undoubtedly does play a part. Looked at in one way, it does not express any ethical idea at all, but merely asserts what *are* the natural consequences of certain activities: 'whatsoever a man soweth, that shall he also reap'; 'the sins of the fathers shall be visited upon the children'; this is the way of the world. But an ethical connotation is liable to attach itself to the use of the expressions 'a right' and 'deserves', and even to the prophetic 'shall'. Such ethical connotation may or may not be justified.

So far as evil consequences are concerned, to say that a man 'deserves' the results of his natural defects (e.g., of his ignorance, stupidity, or clumsiness), would generally be regarded, to the extent that the use of the word 'deserves' conveys an ethical connotation, as itself an *immoral* judgement. This would not be true if we thought that the extent of the defect was in part due to a failure to exercise effort at improvement; then the 'desert' would attach to that failure and not strictly to the defective capacity. Likewise, the ethical connotation of the statement that enterprise 'deserves' its 'reward' may in part express approval of the effort that has been involved. More prominent, however, is the idea that the 'rewards' of such activities are natural consequences which ought not to be interfered with. There would be little point in saying that a Robinson Crusoe 'deserved' the benefits of his ingenuity, for there was no-one to propose interference with his enjoyment of them. Were a man solitary, it would be futile to say, in Hobbesian fashion, that he had a 'right' to such satisfactions as he could achieve. We assert his 'right' only when there is someone else who might propose to deny him the enjoyment of the natural consequences of his activity. In then asserting his 'right' (or claim) we assert an obligation on the part of others not to interfere, and this is again the claim of liberty. The 'just' rewards of enterprise depend in part on utility and in part on the idea of moral protection for the unhindered use by an individual of the advantageous capacities with which he has been endowed. Again the claim of justice and the claim of liberty coincide.

§4. *Equality*

I turn next to the claim of equality. The first difficulty is to decide whether there is any valid principle of equality. Nobody in his senses would say that the alleged claim to equality is a claim that all men *are* equal. The first of the 'truths' that are 'held to be self-evident' by the American Declaration of Independence is 'that all men are born equal'. Similarly the

French Declaration of the Rights of Man, promulgated in 1789, begins: 'Men are born free and equal'. 'Rubbish!' retorts the realist who cannot recognize a metaphor when he sees one. 'Ivan Ivanovitch is born with poor physique, poor brains, poor parents, and as a slave of the Soviet Government; Henry Ford junior is born with good physique, good brains, a millionaire father, and as a free citizen of the free-enterprise U.S.A.' Locke and Rousseau, the Pilgrim Fathers and the French Revolutionaries, the drafters and the signatories of the U.N.O. Declaration of Human Rights, all knew perfectly well that men are not born equal in endowments, possessions, or opportunities. What they and their declarations say is that men are equal 'in respect of their *rights*', i.e., that in some sense men have a claim to equality, not that they *are* equal.

It may be said that a claim to equality must depend on an existing equality. If men have a claim to be considered or treated equally, this can only be because they are already equal in some respect which involves an obligation to treat them equally in action affecting them. It is often held that the claim to equality depends on religious doctrine and is an illustration of the fact that the whole of morality does. The ideals of liberty, equality, and fraternity, that have made themselves felt in western civilization since the French Revolution, owe their origin, it is claimed, to the religion of the Bible and rest on its doctrine. That they originated with the religious doctrine I think we may admit. Whether they can logically be derived from it is more dubious.

The justification for equal treatment despite natural inequality, it is said, is the fact that, in religious doctrine, we are all the children of God and are therefore brothers. But does this metaphor help? It says that I should treat every man as I treat my brothers, i.e., as love would prompt, and it wishes to persuade me that this is my obligation by affirming that, morally and religiously though not biologically, all men are my brothers; moral conduct towards other men, i.e., my obligation to them, is therefore the same in content as my natural conduct to my natural brothers. But does a man always love each of his brothers *equally?* Or as much as he may love one or two of his friends, or his wife, or his children? His children—there, it might be said, is the point. God loves us all as his children, and he loves us equally. For if you ask a parent which of his children he loves best, he will tell you that he loves each of them equally. This is not always true; did not Jacob love Joseph best? But even if it is true, does it follow that because a father loves each of his children equally, they will love each other equally? No, it will be replied, but they *should*. But then we have not been given a reason for the obligation. The doctrine of the fatherhood of God and the consequent brotherhood of man was supposed to tell us *why* we should love each other equally. It was to do this by giving us reason to regard those who are not literally our brothers as if they were. The use of the image, however, does not necessarily convey with it the idea of equality. Where a group of people are literally of the same family, they may think that they *ought* to act with equal love to each of their brethren, but their kinship does not necessarily cause them to do so nor does it give them a reason why they ought to do so. A man may consider both that he has an obligation to treat his brothers equally and that he has an obligation to treat all men equally, but he may still ask why in *each* of the two cases. The fact that he and his brothers have a common parent who loves each of them equally, seems irrelevant.

There is a further difficulty in the view that the doctrine of the fatherhood of God justifies the moral principle of equality. If the obligation arises from the fact that we are all creatures of God, who loves equally all his handiwork, then does he not bear equal love to the animals, who are also his creatures? Does it then follow that we should treat all life (or indeed all existent things) equally with men? Some Indian mystics have apparently thought that we should have an equal regard for insects to that which we have for men. There is a sect, we are told, who carefully brush to the side of the path before them as they walk, lest they might tread on some minute insects. But why stop at insects? If equal respect for the creation of God is the fundamental rule, must we not likewise avoid the destruction of vegetable matter? Yet if we do not devour some living things, we shall not live.

The religious doctrine so far considered, then, does not give a basis for the claim to equality. But perhaps we have not seized upon the crucial element in the doctrine. It may be argued that the principle of equality rests on the fact that all men are born equal as moral agents, as having the dignity of a moral being, i.e. of the capacity to be moral, and thus they are equal in the sight of God. Other theologians, I have been told, interpret 'equality in the sight of God' as equality in sin; we are all born equally steeped in original sin. Whether or not we accept the latter interpretation of 'equality in the sight of God', it is of course true that all men are potential moral agents and therefore have an equal 'dignity' not possessed by beings incapable of morality. But this equality is not what an enslaved or downtrodden populace refers to in claiming equality of rights. The 'rights' or claims of justice are claims to *happiness* (or the opportunity to pursue happiness, or the means to happiness). Nobody would say that the equality of all men as potential moral agents involves equal claims to happiness, and it is to be hoped that the upholders of original sin do not think that all men have equal claims to misery, that they are all *equally* damned. If we are to consider the relation between our *moral* natures and our claims to happiness, it seems more reasonable to say that moral achievement, not mere potentiality, is what counts in determining 'rights' or claims; the non-egalitarian principle of desert supplies the connecting link.

It is for this reason that some moralists would deny the validity of any positive claim to equality. If men are equal only in moral potentiality, and if claims to happiness are determined by moral achievement, in which men are unequal, how can we say they have equal claims? Accordingly, it may be held, the principle of desert is the sole principle of 'distributive justice' and there is no claim to equal distribution apart from this. 'Distributive justice', the argument would run, following Aristotle, is a distribution according to merit; unequal shares to unequals, and equal shares to equals. Equal distribution is right only when there is equal desert.

To sustain this view, we must interpret 'desert' or 'merit' widely, including the sense discussed in §3 as well as that of §2. Inequality, whether of liberty, wealth, opportunity, or other desirable things, may be justified by differences of moral merit, of economic 'merit', or of natural 'merit'. A man who has wilfully committed a crime deserves to be imprisoned; an enterprising manufacturer 'deserves' the fruits of his success; a bright child 'deserves' a good education. Taking 'merit' or 'desert' in this wide sense, it may be claimed that just distribution is always in accordance with merit.

Then what are we to say of claims to equality? That these, when justified, are always based on equal merit? This suggestion would cover only a proportion of the relevant instances. It may be held, however, that claims to equality are usually to be interpreted negatively as justified protests against particular inequalities, justified not because there is any positive claim to equality but because the inequality is not 'deserved', i.e., has an improper ground. It is unjust that Aristides be selected for ostracism; that a businessman become rich by 'profiteering', that is, by making large profits in circumstances in which the general interest is harmed by his 'enterprise'; that a dull witted Vere de Vere be selected for Eton in preference to a bright Smith. The ground of the particular inequality attacked is morally 'irrelevant', while an existing 'relevant' ground for differentiation is ignored. The objection is not to inequality as such but to the ground of differentiation. The unequal treatment has conflicted with merit, where 'merit' can mean moral worth, social utility, or natural capacity. In these respects men are of unequal 'worth', and their treatment or status, it may be held, should be in accordance with their different 'worths'. But throughout history unequal treatment has almost always far exceeded, or cut across, the differences of 'worth'. Some men are of lesser 'worth' than others, but none are so much less valuable than others that they should be their serfs, still less their slaves or chattels. Even where those treated as of less account have not been serfs but just a lower class, the higher class has seldom consisted of those who are more 'worthy' in virtue, utility, or capacity; usually, membership of the privileged class has been based on birth or similar accidents. Accordingly, the argument might conclude, the cry for equality is really a cry against unjustified inequality; but if, *per impossibile,* human affairs could be so arranged that men were treated in accordance with their natural inequalities, all would be well. To treat them equally, however, when they are naturally unequal, is just as wrong as to exaggerate or to run directly counter to their natural inequalities.

This view smacks of the 'aristocrat', the 'superior person', and therefore in these days many of us have a prejudice against it. But it cannot be easily dismissed, and the difficulty of justifying a positive claim to equality in the face of natural inequality tempts one to think that it must be true. Further, it need not in practice lead to aristocracy. For a modern exponent of the theory may agree that if, like Plato, we try to adjust our human affairs to the degree of inequality conferred on men by nature, we shall be sure to make a mess of it. The advice that the theory might offer for practice is this: 'We should neither try to secure equality nor try to adjust treatment to nature. Both are impracticable. What we should do, and what successful reformers have in fact done, is to protest against and remove unjustified inequality, inequality that clearly goes against the inequalities of nature. If we stick to this task, we shall have plenty to do, and shall not be led into extravagant and impracticable paths.'

As practical advice, I think this is sensible; and the view does contain a great part of the truth about equality. Where the cry for equality has reference to the claims of 'worth', i.e., of moral merit, natural capacity, or social utility, it is not based on a positive belief in equality but is a negative plea against unjustified inequality. To this extent the claim to equality is negative.

But the theory, as expounded so far, omits one of the

justifying grounds for unequal treatment, and this ground, paradoxical though it appears at first sight, points to a limited positive claim to equality. Unequal treatment may be justified, not only on account of the different 'worths' of the recipients, but also on account of their different needs. We think it right to make special provision for those affected by special needs, through natural disability, such as mental or physical weakness, or through the slings and arrows of outrageous fortune, through sickness, unemployment, or destitute old age. Here, it would seem, we go *against* nature, and think ourselves justified in doing so. The unequal treatment meted out is in *inverse* proportion to natural inequalities. We attempt to remedy, so far as we can, the inequality of nature. Though in the mere provision of aid, monetary or other, we seem at first sight to do more for the needy person than for the normal, to make an unequal discrimination in favour of the former, the inequality of treatment is an attempt to reduce the existing inequality, to bring the needy person up to the same level of advantages as the normal. We try to make up for the natural inequality and to give the handicapped, so far as possible, equal opportunities and equal satisfactions to those possessed by the non-handicapped. We think that they have a claim to this, that we are obliged to bring them up to equality with the normal, deliberately to go against the inequalities of nature.

It is, however, an exaggeration to say, without qualification, that justice here is a matter of going against nature. For in dealing with the handicaps with which some people are born, we usually cannot provide them with fully equal opportunities to those possessed by normal people. We can try, as the theory we are considering bids us, to see that their handicap is not allowed, by the social arrangements of man, to extend beyond what it naturally must be. In the past, for example, handicapped children were neglected while normal children were, for reasons of utility, given opportunity for development. We think that we ought to remedy the neglect, to give the handicapped child such opportunities for development as his natural capacities allow. We try to ensure that the inequalities of nature are not exaggerated, but we cannot remove the natural inequalities themselves.

Yet it would be a mistake to think that, because some natural handicaps cannot be removed, there is no obligation to remove those which we can. If we can cure congenital blindness, we think we have an obligation to do so. We do not think that illness should simply be left to take its natural course; sometimes 'leaving it to nature' is the best way to cure illness, sometimes not, and we think we ought to take the course, natural or not, which will be most likely to effect the cure. Where a person's peculiar disadvantages are due to external causes, such as an economic slump, an earthquake, or a flood, we certainly think that we should remedy them and, if possible, prevent them.

The claim of need, then, involves a distribution not in accordance with existing differences but contrary to them. People do of course differ in their needs, so that the provision of satisfaction for them will be an unequal one. But strictly, the potential needs and desires of people, even the most fortunate, are unlimited. Although I have not the special need of an invalid for eggs, I could do with quite a lot. Although normal children do not have the special need of the handicapped child for special educational equipment and personal supervision, they could quite well do with better educational equipment and more personal supervision than they now receive. How do we determine when a need is a 'special' one? Our recognition of 'special' needs is a recognition that some persons, by reasons of nature or accident, fall below the normal level of satisfactions, below the level which most people enjoy and which we regard as essential for decent living. Our attempt to meet these special needs is an attempt to bring such people up to the normal level of satisfactions, or as near to it as we can. When we do more for the handicapped child or the disabled man, this is a recognition that they are at present unequal to (below) most people in capacity to earn their living and have a reasonably happy life. Our unequal (greater) provision of care for them is an attempt to reduce the existing inequality; we want, so far as we can, to bring them to a level of equality with others in capacity to enjoy their lives. Thus the basis of the claim of special need is really a recognition of a claim to equality. It is a positive moral claim taking its place with others such as the claims of moral worth, utility, and capacity. For note that this claim of need remains even if there is no other moral claim. The permanently disabled, the aged, the insane, have, we think, a claim to be taken care of, to a reasonable measure of comfort and happiness, even though they are incapable of making any return. Satisfaction of the claim may conflict with social utility; these people are a burden on society, yet we think the claim should be met.

§5. *Equality and liberty*

Having established that there is a positive claim to equality, let us now consider more directly its content. In the course of this examination, I shall inquire also whether, as is often alleged, the claim of equality conflicts with that of liberty. Many people who would agree that the principle of desert may go hand in hand with the claims of liberty would deny that liberty is compatible with equality. *Prima facie* at least, there would seem to be a conflict between the principle of equality on the one side and the principles of liberty and desert on the other.

To what precisely do we regard people as having an equal claim? Equality of what? Of consideration, of opportunity, of material goods, or of happiness? Certainly to equality of consideration; i.e., we recognize the right of *everyone* to have his various claims considered. But this is only a way of saying that everyone *has* claims; it does not involve any additional content as the claim of distributive justice. We also recognize a claim to equality of opportunity, that is, a claim of every man to an equal chance of developing his capacities and pursuing his interests. Is there also a claim to equal distribution? That is, when material means to happiness are available, should they, in the absence of other claims, be distributed equally? The question may be put alternatively thus: Have men a claim to equal happiness, or only to an equal chance of pursuing happiness?

In fact, of course, equal happiness cannot be secured. If, for instance, everyone were given the same amount of money, the different tastes of different persons, and the different costs of satisfying their tastes, would mean that the same amount of money would provide more happiness for some than for others; if I like beer and you like whisky, I should be able to say '*Nunc est bibendum*' more often than you. Again, some would, by luck or greater ability, soon turn their standard income into a larger one, while others would soon be paupers. However, this practical impossibility of providing equal happiness does not affect the theoretical question. For many obligations cannot in practice be fully satisfied. If, for example, it be held that we have an obligation to increase the sum of happiness or good, or to distribute happiness in accordance with merit, this is in practice often impossible. The relevant obligation is really to try to aim at or approach the proposed ideal. The question is, whether the proposed ideal of equal happiness is a legitimate one. It seems to conflict with the ideal of equal opportunity, for if that is given full rein then different abilities will result in different degrees of success in pursuing happiness. A conflict between two principles does not necessarily mean that one of them is illegitimate, for all claims may conflict with each other. But the conflict may lead some people to deny the validity of one of the principles because they feel clearly bound by the other. A consideration of what each involves will help to show just where the apparent conflict lies and whether it is really, as appears on the surface, between the claims of equal opportunity and equal happiness.

Let us first see what is involved in 'equality of opportunity'. I think that this is bound up with the idea of liberty. The idea of liberty is, primarily, a negative one, the removal of restraints upon doing what one wishes. Such restraints may be imposed by the actions of other persons or may be due to natural obstacles. Social liberty refers to the removal of restraints by other persons. The restraints of nature may be external or internal. The Firth of Clyde prevents me from walking to Bute, and if I wish to get to Bute a ferry must be provided. But besides such external obstacles to the satisfaction of our desires, there are also internal restraints. If I want to be a champion tennis-player, I am restrained by the weakness of my sight. Of internal restraints, some can be removed, others cannot. I have not the natural endowment to become a good tennis-player, but I have the natural endowment to become a fair chess-player. Natural endowments, however, cannot always be exercised by their possessor without training and suitable environment; in the absence of these, they remain unfulfilled potentialities. My potential capacity to become a fair chess-player is subject to the natural restraint that, if left to itself without training and practice, it cannot be actualized. Suitable training and practice are the removal of the natural restraint on the exercise of natural potentialities. Two children may have the potentiality of becoming good craftsmen. If one is given the necessary training and suitable environment to enable him to develop his potentialities so as to lead a satisfying life and to be socially useful, he thereby receives opportunity to make the most of his capacities. If the other is not given such training, he is denied the opportunity to make the most of his capacities. Equal opportunity means, ideally, maximum opportunity for all to develop the potentialities they have, and failing that, the maximum that is possible in the face of, e.g., economic difficulties. The opportunity is to be equally, i.e. impartially, spread, in the sense that discrimination in the provision of a particular type of opportunity for some and not for others should depend on the potentialities that the prospective recipients have, instead of depending on 'irrelevant' considerations such as birth or wealth.

Social liberty, we said, is the absence of restraint by other persons. The provision of opportunity, however, involves, not the absence of action by other persons, but its presence in the form of aid and training in the development of capacities.

Liberal political philosophy concentrated on social liberty. But the mere absence of interference by others does not give full opportunities to all to pursue happiness in accordance with their capacities, because many capacities do not develop of themselves but need assistance. When Mill rests the claim to liberty on the value of 'the development of individuality', he implies an extension of the old Liberal idea of liberty. It would be generally agreed by thoughtful people to-day that men have a moral claim not only to social liberty but also to liberty in the further sense of maximum development of potentiality. 'Equality' of opportunity simply means the provision of maximum opportunity to *all,* in place of the denial of opportunity to some for extraneous reasons. But if all men are given maximum opportunity for development, this will not result in equal happiness, for they differ in their potentialities so that some will be more able than others to achieve happiness for themselves by the exercise of their developed capacities.

Let us now turn to the other suggested principle of equal satisfactions. There seems to be some claim that all should be given equal satisfactions to the extent that this is within our power, e.g., in the provision of material means to happiness. This principle would conflict with the principle of maximum opportunity for all, if the latter were taken to imply, not only that a man should be enabled to develop his potentialities to the fullest extent, but also that he should be allowed to use his developed capacities as he wishes for his own maximum enjoyment. The second of these two implications is required by the principle of social liberty, and the two together by a combination of the principle of maximum opportunity with the principle of social liberty. The principle of opportunity alone, however, need not necessarily be held to conflict with the principle of equal satisfactions, for a man might be enabled to develop his capacities but be required to devote the fruits of his capacities to the common good; that is to say, he might be expected to retain or receive, for his own enjoyment, a roughly equal amount of material means to satisfaction as others, while any surplus material results of his exercise of capacity were distributed to others whose own capacities did not allow them to effect as much. This is the egalitarian position—from each according to his capacity, to each according to his needs. The position conflicts with the principle of maximum social liberty, but not with the principle of maximum opportunity.

In practice, however, neither the position of extreme Liberalism nor the position of extreme egalitarianism is acceptable in isolation. The egalitarian has to give some weight to social liberty for the sake of utility, that is, in order to provide incentives to production so that the needs which can be satisfied may be at a maximum. There is in fact no limit to the desires which can be satisfied, so that distribution 'to each according to his needs' must always be below what could be done. Accordingly, certain desires, which are thought to be more fundamental than others, are distinguished by the name of 'needs', and it is thought that these should be satisfied for all equally before further desires are satisfied for any. 'Bread for all before there is jam for some.' The jam, however, is not distributed equally. On the other hand, the Liberal position is rarely carried to the extreme conclusion, 'Each for himself and devil take the hindmost'. Few adherents of the position would be content to let the weak and the aged starve to death. Some sort of basic minimum, ranging from the paltry assistance of the Poor Law to the ambitions of the 'Beveridge Programme', is usually admitted, and this is a concession to the principle of equal satisfactions. Justice is thought to require a basic minimum of equal satisfactions, unrelated to utility or to capacity. Above that line, room is left for individuals to do as they think fit. The position of the line is different in different societies and at different periods of history, depending both on economic circumstances and on the level of social morality. That it depends on economic circumstances is obvious enough. 'A chicken in every pot' is impossible if a country cannot afford to raise or buy enough chickens. But it depends on the level of social morality, too. Tom Paine proposed in 1797 the establishment of a national fund, from which everyone should receive £15 at the age of twenty-one and £10 at the age of fifty 'to enable them to live without wretchedness and go decently out of the world'.[1] The country could have afforded this very limited scheme of 'social security', depending as it did, like the Beveridge plan, on some redistribution of existing income; but most of the people who could influence social legislation at the time would have thought it wildly utopian. On the other hand, many of our contemporaries would say that the Labour Government of 1945-1951, in sticking to all the benefits of the Welfare State irrespective of whether the country could then afford them, allowed its moral fervour to outrun economic necessity.

Distributive justice, we have found, makes two claims of equality, first, equality of opportunity, that is, the greatest possible degree of opportunity for all impartially; and second, the provision of material means to satisfaction for all impartially, such provision in practice being limited, for utilitarian reasons, to a standard of basic needs.

The first of these principles depends partly on utility (since the development and exercise of a good many capacities is useful for the production of means to satisfaction for society at large), and partly on valuing self-development. This implies that the development of capacity is regarded as a moral claim, reinforced by the claim of utility if the capacity is especially useful to society (as, e.g., technical skill or teaching ability is, and the capacity for playing chess is not), and overridden by the claim of utility if the capacity is socially harmful (e.g., the capacity for burglary; we do not think we ought to provide schools of burglary for potentially successful burglars). Since people differ in capacities, and since some men are better endowed than others with a particular capacity, this claim for the development of capacity is not one for equality (except in the sense that it is a claim of everyone) but reflects the differences of nature. We speak of '*equal* opportunity' because, in

[1]*Agrarian Justice;* quoted by Maitland in *Liberty and Equality* (*Collected Papers,* Vol. I, p. 148).

the past, the opportunities provided for development have not been in accordance with the inequalities of nature, but have either run counter to them for the private interests of some or else exaggerated them for the sake of general interest. Where opportunity was not confined to privilege, it depended on social utility; it was extended to those whose development would benefit society to an unusual degree. Thus there is no need to invoke justice in order to approve of the provision of free higher education for the gifted children of poor parents; social utility will require it no less. But the provision of equal opportunity for the handicapped, in mind or body, can often not be justified by utility. It is true that a disabled man trained is more useful than untrained. But if the cost of his training were greater than his potential utility, we should still think ourselves obliged, for *his* sake, to provide the training if we could. It may be true that the expense to society of training him for an uneconomic return is a lesser burden than supporting him untrained, but if utility alone determined our attitude society could rid itself of all burden by letting him starve.

The second element of distributive justice ensures that there is a basic minimum for all even if some of those affected could not achieve it by their own efforts. Here we 'go against nature' in the sense that we rate basic needs above the capacity to satisfy them, and of course above social utility, for keeping alive the aged and the incurably sick is not economic. We think it is due to *them* as individuals.

The two principles of equality, like the principle of retributive justice, are chiefly concerned to protect the individual irrespective of general utility. One is a claim that each person be given such opportunity for development as his natural capacity allows, even though it may not always add to social utility (but we shall do still more for socially useful capacities because of their utility). The other is a claim for the satisfaction of basic needs (i.e. those regarded as essential for tolerable living) for each individual even though there may be no economic return. We think these two things are due to individuals as such, as being 'ends-in-themselves'. If, with Mill, we hold that the most important element in the idea of liberty is not the negative factor of the absence of restraint but the positive factor of valuing individuality, then the essential point of justice and that of liberty are the same.

VI

LOGIC OF MORALS AND METAPHYSIC OF MORALS

Our discussion of justice has confirmed the view, suggested in Chapter III, that the deontologists' picture of the logic of moral principles covers the moral judgements of common sense more closely than does any version of utilitarianism. But we have also seen that the deontologists' formulations of their system go beyond common-sense thought in precision and clarity. This is true even at the level of about half-a-dozen principles, such as are given by Richard Price, Sir David Ross, and Dr. Carritt, and more obviously so at the level of two or three general classes of principles suggested by Ross and Carritt. We observed that the differences between the classifications of individual theorists, either at the less or at the more general level, could not be resolved simply by consideration of common-sense judgements. All go beyond common sense, and all are more or less permitted by common sense. That is, they are all permissible systematizations; none conflict violently in their implications with common-sense judgements, in the way that utilitarian systems do at some points.

In the metaphysic of morals we wish to carry farther, if we can, the process of synthesis. Obviously this cannot be done merely by a systematic presentation of common-sense moral judgement, for we have already gone beyond that at the two levels of systematization mentioned just now. The logic of morals, produced from reflection on ordinary moral judgements, *suggests* that a further degree of coherence must exist. If only two basic ethical concepts are involved, and if there is (as there seems to be) some relation between those two concepts, then it should be possible to show some similar connexion between the principles which employ ethical concepts. Such a connexion, if it is to be found, may fairly be said to be presupposed by ordinary moral judgements, but our discussion of the logic of morals has shown that the connexion cannot be reached directly from an examination of moral judgements themselves.

The logic of morals considers the logical relationships implicit in the intentional meaning of moral judgements, in what persons making such judgements assert. A consideration of intentional meaning cannot give us any greater coherence than that shown in the deontological systems. If we are to unify the moral system we must no longer confine ourselves to what moral judgements assert. We must consider, if we can, not simply what is asserted but what are the facts. We must step outside logic to metaphysics. We cannot usefully pursue any farther the question: What do judgements of, e.g., obligation say? We must ask instead: What is the nature of obligation? To what facts does talk of obligation refer? To what facts does talk of fittingness (or goodness) refer? And what is the relation between the first and the second? Such an inquiry is liable to be in some degree speculative. Once we step outside the intentional meaning of common-sense judgement, there is no safe criterion of what 'the facts', for our particular purpose, are. The extrinsic test to be satisfied by a metaphysical theory is that of permitting (when the relevant empirical premisses are added) the deduction of the data with which we began, in this case the moral judgements of common sense. The intrinsic test is the success of the theory in unifying the manifold. The reason for pursuing a metaphysical theory, instead of just accepting the initial data and what can be derived immediately from them, is simply the urge of the human intellect to synthesize.

My procedure, in discussing the metaphysic of morals, will be to use a system of the logic of morals similar to the systems of Ross and Carritt, and to try to suggest some unifying principle or concept from which the various principles of the system can be derived. I shall assume that the preceding argument of Part I has shown my proposed system of the logic of morals to be in accordance with the moral judgements of common sense, and therefore that a metaphysical theory which is adequate for the system is also adequate for the initial data.

In this chapter, I propose to set out the system of the logic of morals that I shall use for this purpose. I shall give two alternative classifications of right acts. The first follows the general pattern of Sir David Ross's classification, the second that of Dr. Carritt. There will be differences of detail, but I think that my formulations are permitted by common-sense moral judgements to about the same degree as are those of Ross and Carritt. My classifications will distinguish between obligation and fittingness as proposed in my logic of moral concepts. To some extent this is only a verbal matter. But in places it involves differences of substance. The individual deontologists are not always agreed on the acceptance or rejection of particular principles. For instance, both Sir David Ross and Dr. Carritt accept a principle of obligation to realize intrinsic good as such. Professor Prichard (if I understand him aright) did not. I have stated that I reject it as a principle of obligation but accept it as a principle of fitting action. Another example is the question whether the pursuit of one's own happiness is obligatory, a question to which Ross gives a negative answer, as I do, while Carritt gives it a hesitantly affirmative answer. On these matters I have offered some argument for my views in Chapter IV. The reasons why I adopt my own classifications of right acts rather than the classifications of Ross and Carritt are, first, because mine appear to me to be closer to my own moral thinking, and secondly, because I think, rightly or wrongly, that my formulations allow a unifying concept to become more easily apparent. As with the systems of Ross and Carritt at the more general of the two levels which they employ, my divisions will give a small number of generic classes of right action, under which will be subsumed specific classes corresponding to the lower-level principles commonly asserted by deontologists.

First classification

A: Acts whose moral character is of general incidence, i.e.

is not determined by the specific character of specific situations.

(1) Acts generally obligatory, i.e. obligatory upon all moral agents, and obligatory towards all persons (or, where relevant, persons and other sensitive creatures) whom they may affect by their action.
   (i) Non-interference with the liberty of others to pursue their desires where these raise no moral issue.
   (ii) Relief of pain, and refraining from giving pain.
   (iii) Veracity or non-deceit.
   (iv) Treatment on a basis of equality.

(2) Acts generally fitting, i.e. fitting for all occasions.
   (i) Increasing happiness.
   (ii) Producing other good states of mind, namely virtue, knowledge, and the creation and appreciation of beauty.

B: Acts whose moral character is of specific incidence, i.e. is determined by the specific character of specific situations. The moral character so arising is that of obligation, so that the acts in question are acts of specific obligation. Specific obligation differs from obligation of general incidence in that it arises from special relations between particular persons. These relations may be due, first, to individual past acts, whether of the agent, of the claimant, or of both; or secondly, to a more continuous association between them.

(1) Obligations arising from individual past acts.
   (i) Past acts of the agent give rise to the obligations of reparation and of promise-keeping.
   (ii) Past acts of the claimant give rise to the obligations of rewarding merit and of gratitude for benefits.
   (iii) Past acts of both parties give rise to the obligation of fulfilling contracts.

(2) Obligations arising from association between

particular persons. These are the obligations arising from love and friendship, and in general the obligations of loyalty to a person or group with whom or with which one has had a continuous association.

It will be seen that there are two general distinctions drawn here, (*a*) between acts whose moral character is of general incidence and those whose moral character is of specific incidence, and (*b*) between obligatory acts and fitting acts. These distinctions are of equal generality, so that the main outline of the scheme could have been set out thus:

A: Obligatory acts
(1) of general incidence,
(2) of specific incidence.
B: Fitting acts
of general incidence.

These two distinctions, which form the skeleton of the first classification, relate to the kind of moral character possessed by a right act, and to its degree of 'spread'.

Second classification

The alternative scheme, which is simpler, makes the main line of distinction between what we are to produce by our act, and (in the case of obligations) for whom we are to produce it.

A: Beneficence

Right acts are intended to produce good, i.e. happiness (the satisfaction of desires) and other good states of mind, or to remove, and refrain from producing, evil, i.e. unhappiness and other bad states of mind. That is to say, all right acts are *at least* fitting.

B: Justice and friendship

The claims of justice and friendship determine our obligations, i.e., they determine for whom we are obliged to do what is in any circumstances fitting. These claims are as follows:

(1) The general claims of distributive justice that those whom we may affect by our action be

treated on a basis of equality in the absence of special considerations.

(i) The claim of equal liberty, i.e. that everyone be permitted without interference to pursue his legitimate ends, and be free from the deliberate infliction of evil.

(ii) The claim of equal opportunity, i.e. that everyone be positively enabled to pursue good in accordance with his capacity.

(iii) The claim of equal satisfactions, i.e. that everyone be delivered from, and made secure against, evil, at least up to a 'standard level' of satisfactions.

(2) Specific claims depending on special considerations.

(i) The claims of retributive justice. These are the claims of reparation, gratitude, and desert.

(ii) The claims of commutative justice. This covers the obligations of promises and contracts.

(iii) The claims of love, friendship, and association generally.

The distinction, under *B*, between general and special claims corresponds to the distinction in the first classification between obligations of general incidence and obligations of specific incidence. With one possible exception, it will be clear how all the classes of acts mentioned in the first classification are covered by the second classification. The possible exception is the obligation to veracity. The satisfaction of desires, mentioned under 'beneficence', includes the desire to know, implied in the asking of a question, and the giving of a truthful answer is therefore an instance of producing good. It is of course also a general obligation owed equally to all, and in that respect falls under distributive justice, as do all obligations of general incidence. I should say that it falls under claim (i) of distributive justice. To lie is deliberately to inflict evil. Like all deliberate infliction of evil, it impedes liberty. The prevalence of deliberately deceitful propaganda is one reason (though only one of many reasons) why a totalitarian society is not a free society.

It should be needless to add that all the specifications of obligatory and fitting action are limited by two qualifications. First, they are all to be understood as having attached to them the provisoes 'if one can' and 'as far as one can'. Secondly, any instance of a principle of obligation may conflict with and be overridden by one or more instances of other principles of obligation; and any instance of a class of fitting acts may conflict with and be overridden by one or more instances either of a fitting or of an obligatory class of acts.

The tasks that remain to be undertaken in what I am calling the metaphysic of morals are as follows:

(1) We must try to simplify or unify the moral system so far as possible, to show some connexion between its different principles and concepts so that their presence together becomes more intelligible. In doing this, we are forced to go beyond the direct *meaning* of moral judgements, the content of the thought of moral agents in making them. We must bring out what is presupposed, rather than what is asserted, by moral judgement.

(2) Having outlined the presuppositions of morality as we know it, the metaphysic of morals should consider the relationship of this system of morality to alternative systems. These might be systems actually found in use elsewhere, or they might be constructed abstractly by reflection on the archetypal idea or ideas of the system familiar to us and on the possibility of using some other leading idea as the foundation for guidance in action. We must then see if we can find any rational considerations whereby we may compare these alternative systems with our own and with each other, and whereby we may pronounce in favour of one as somehow superior to the rest. No doubt we shall be predisposed to try to justify our own as the superior one, and it would be foolish to suppose

that we shall be able to make our comparative assessment with complete impartiality. Still, the attempt to find a rational ground for assessment is likely to weaken in some degree the natural prejudice in favour of our own standards, and that has always been a worth-while task for philosophy.

(3) We must also consider whether the presuppositions of our system are consistent with the presuppositions of systematic thought in other fields (e.g., of natural science). If there are inconsistencies, and if the system of thought that clashes with the moral system seems on other grounds to be well established, we must try to reconcile the clash, or, if need be, we must decide that one of the bodies of thought so clashing must be rejected as untrue because inconsistent with what is taken to be true. We might in the end have to decide that either moral thinking, or else another body of human thought, is based on an illusion because the two are incompatible with each other.

PART TWO

METAPHYSIC OF MORALS

VII

A THEORY OF MORAL OBLIGATION

§1. *A condition of moral obligation*

The idea of obligation is applied only to rational beings. Why exactly is this so? 'Ought' implies 'can', and only a rational being, we think, has freedom of choice. But this is not the sole reason. In order to be a moral agent a person must be capable of *recognizing* the claims of morality. This is puzzling. It seems to imply that he must recognize the obligation before he can have it, before it is there to be recognized. Or is the position rather that he must be aware of something else in order to have an obligation? Then what is this something else, and in particular, what is there in the facts giving rise to a moral obligation that is additional to, or different from, the facts of apparently similar situations where we do not speak of any moral attributes arising?

Consider our judgements about animals in circumstances analogous to moral situations. Hume[1] asks why we do not attribute virtue and vice to animals and to vegetation. We condemn Nero for murdering his mother, but if a tiger kills another creature or if a sapling overtops and destroys its parent tree we do not use moral language about them. This is one of Hume's strongest arguments for the subjectivity of moral terms. The word 'vice', he concludes, can only refer to something in the spectator who makes the judgement that Nero's act was vicious; it refers to the spectator's feeling of disapproval.

But we may still ask, on Hume's own positive theory of ethics, why we do not feel disapproval on observing, or hearing about, a tiger's cruelty, or why we do not feel approval, of the

[1] *Treatise of Human Nature,* Book III, Part I, section i; *Enquiry concerning the Principles of Morals,* Appendix I.

sort we should express for a dutiful parent, when we observe an animal following its maternal instinct in fostering its young. Hume holds that approval of an act is, or arises from, a combination of (1) sympathy with the person affected by the act, and (2) the thought of the general utility of acts of that kind; for disapproval, the two factors are (1) sympathy with the person affected, and (2) thought of general harmfulness. Accordingly, when we approve of a parent for taking care of his child, we are sympathizing with the happiness received by the child and are thinking of the general utility of parental care. When we disapprove of Nero's act of parricide, we are feeling sympathy for his victim and are thinking of the general harm wrought by murder. Now abstract the features which, according to Hume, are the morally relevant features of these situations. How do they differ from our reactions to the maternal instinct of animals and to the cruelty of tigers? We may feel sympathy for the creature affected by its parent's maternal instinct or by the tiger's cruelty, and we may think the maternal instinct useful and the cruelty harmful to sensitive creatures generally (and possibly to man). It would follow, if Hume's theory were true, that we should feel approval of the bird that fosters its young no less than of Agrippina for fostering Nero, and that we should feel disapproval of the tiger that rends a goat no less than of Nero for murdering his mother. We may indeed have towards the bird and the tiger feelings that could be called a kind of approval and disapproval, but we should not normally say that the bird acts as it ought and the tiger as it ought not, that the one is morally good and the other morally bad. Hume himself does not want to say that we feel moral approval and disapproval towards animals. His earlier objection rested on the fact that we do not call animals or trees virtuous and vicious. But his own positive theory provides no solution to the difficulty of explaining why we do not pass moral judgements on animals in situations analogous to those in which we pass moral judgements on men. If moral judgement were all that he says it is, there would be no relevant difference in the two kinds of situation.

I have argued that moral obligations are always *to* other beings. If this be granted, the solution to Hume's difficulty lies in the fact that the ideas of moral obligation and of moral goodness and badness apply only where there can be an imaginative awareness by the agent of conations and affections in another creature. (There is also the condition, mentioned at the beginning of this discussion, that the agent must be capable of free choice.) The tendency of a plant to grow is not a conation proper, since the plant has no consciousness, as we suppose. Consequently we do not think any moral issues arise when we cut down or harm a tree. Such an act may be right or wrong because of its consequences for men, but that is a different matter. Animals, unlike plants, have, we think, conscious feelings and conations. The satisfaction or thwarting of these is thought to have a moral quality, but only if such action is taken by a being who can imagine the animal's feelings and conations. A tiger is not, we suppose, capable of imagining a goat's pain, and is not free to desist from the impulse to kill the goat, and so we do not talk of it as having any obligation. A man can imagine the pain of a rabbit in a trap, and so has an obligation, if he is able, to relieve the pain.

The imaginative awareness of the feelings and desires of other beings, which is a condition of moral obligation, is a sympathetic awareness. It is possible to imagine the feelings of others and be unmoved. The state of mind which I am trying to describe is a compound of imaginative cognition and of affection. It has its conative side, too, though I prefer not to call this a desire, since it is usual to distinguish the motive of obligation from that of 'natural' desire. Hume and Adam Smith were right in regarding sympathy as fundamental to morality. But they conducted their investigation of morality primarily from the point of view of a spectator, speaking of his sympathy with the person affected by the act or with the motives of the agent. Having begun with the reactions of the spectator, Hume and Smith turned later to the state of mind of the agent, and gave an account of that in terms of his reaction to the reactions of spectators. In fact, the sympathy that is central for morality is the sympathy which an *agent* may have for the being whom he can affect by his action. And sympathy is not a bare feeling, as Hume evidently thought, but is, as Adam Smith seems to have realized in developing his theory, a highly complex state of mind involving thought and imagination.

In saying that obligation depends on thought, I am not saying that obligation depends on the thought of obligation, that an agent is obliged because he thinks he is. That would be a vicious circle. Nor am I saying that obligation depends on the thought of a claim, for that would only be a concealed way of repeating the vicious circle. I am saying that an obligation (and therefore a claim) depends on the thought of certain, real or supposed, natural facts which, as we say, give rise to the obligation. If I think that a sensitive creature is in pain and I can help, I am obliged to do so.

If claims, being but the content of obligations, depend on thought, does it follow that a bearer of claims, like a bearer of obligations, must be a rational being? The capacity to have a claim involves on the part of the claimant the existence, and consciousness, of affections and conations, e.g. of a pain and the urge to be rid of it. This affective-conative experience does not become a claim simply in virtue of its existence as a need. If it becomes a claim, it is a claim *upon* a potential agent, who has an obligation to help satisfy the need. The need is a potential or hypothetical claim, i.e. it will become a claim if and when a moral agent is obliged to satisfy it. *Qua* need it is actual, and this is what will involve an obligation, in relevant circumstances, on moral agents capable of recognizing it as a need that they can satisfy; and thereby it will become a claim. The creature that has the need is therefore a potential bearer of claims in virtue (*a*) of having the need and (*b*) of sharing a common world of intercourse with moral agents. Thus we are not required to say that an animal would have to be capable of recognizing claims before it could be a bearer of claims. It is enough if the animal has conscious needs; a creature is a possible bearer of claims if it has conscious conations and affections, i.e., if it consciously feels impulses, and pleasures and pains. For the same reason, we do not have to say that the claims of infants depend on their being potential moral agents, potentially capable of thinking of their own and of others' needs as claims, i.e. as involving obligations for those who can be sympathetically aware of and can satisfy the needs; nor are we required to say in consequence that idiots and animals, not being potential moral agents, can have no claims. We may say in all these cases that such beings can have claims, because they have conscious needs of which a moral agent may be imaginatively aware as claims upon him.

It follows from what has been said, that if a man is not able, or is not in a position, to be aware of another's need, there is no obligation and consequently no claim. What if he mistakenly thinks there is a need? He presumably has an obligation, but has the other party a claim? How can the alleged bearer of a claim have a claim when he has in fact no need and is unconscious of any supposed need? In the mind of the agent, the supposed claimant has a claim; but in the mind of the supposed claimant, there is no claim and hence no obligation. Then if they have contradictory thoughts about the existence or non-existence of an obligation and claim, do the obligation and claim *really* exist or not? My answer is that there are no such things as 'real' obligations and claims apart from people's thoughts. We may ask whether an agent who knew the relevant natural facts of the situation would have an obligation or not, and the answer is plainly that he would not. The actual agent, who falsely believes there is a need, has an obligation. Although the thought giving rise to the obligation is fallible, this does not imply that the obligation is less real than would be the obligation of an agent with infallible knowledge of the relevant facts. Indeed, the supposition of a moral agent having *infallible* knowledge of the relevant facts is illusory. For the relevant facts always include the state of mind of another person or creature whom we can affect by our action; and it is impossible to have infallible knowledge of the state of mind of another. If I had infallible knowledge of another's state of mind, I should be the same person as that other, and (accepting my view that moral obligations are always inter-personal) it would follow that I should have no obligation towards him, for the relation involved would be intra-personal instead of inter-personal.

§2. *The idea of moral obligation*

Let us now return to the classifications of right acts given in our logic of morals. We distinguished between obligatory and fitting acts. Obligations arise only where there are claims, that is, where the agent stands to some other person or persons in a relationship which, in some metaphorical sense, binds them together. Among these, we distinguished between obligations of general incidence and obligations of specific incidence.

Let us look first at acts of specific obligation, where the tie is a particular isolable relationship between two, or a small number of, individuals. I said that these specific obligations arise from particular relations due to past acts, whether of the agent, or of the claimant, or of both, or due to past association between them. Past acts of the agent give rise to the obligations to make reparation for injuries and to keep promises; of the claimant, to the obligations of gratitude and of rewarding merit; of both, to the obligation of fulfilling contracts. Past association gives rise to the obligations of love, friendship, and loyalty generally. The principle of division in distinguishing these four classes of specific obligation lies simply in the source of the relation giving rise to the obligation. The ensuing relations, though they involve different contents of obligation, i.e. different types of acts due, are, *qua* relations, all of the same type. In all four classes, there is an inter-personal tie between agent and claimant, and for the purpose of understanding the idea of obligation the differences in the source of the relation and in the content of the future act required are irrelevant.

If I am aware of having harmed someone (or of having been

benefited by him), I owe him reparation (or gratitude), which is the same as to say that he has a claim to it. My thought of the past act makes for me a mental 'tie' to the other person. A promise is the conscious setting up of an inter-personal tie by pronouncing that some event, the production of which is thought to be within the agent's power, and which will benefit the future claimant, will be brought about by the agent. He thereby gives rise to expectations of benefit from himself and 'binds' himself to fulfil them. Contracts are similar deliberate acts of making moral 'bonds', but differ from one-sided promises in that both parties, each conditionally upon performance by the other, make mutual promises to perform benefits for each other. The obligation to reward merit arises from a realization on the part of the potential agent that the claimant, having acted virtuously, deserves that others should act virtuously towards him; he deserves to be treated as 'an end' even more emphatically than does any man merely *qua* man, for this particular man has acted as a member of 'a realm of ends'. Awareness of his merit is a heightened or emphasized awareness of him as 'an end', i.e. as one whose interests we should satisfy. In all these types of instance, the moral element, the obligation, is constituted by an inter-personal relation, an awareness of oneself as a person in relation to another person, affecting personality by our mutual intercourse. For personality is partly a social product. It is not only the having of cognition and conation and the capacity to satisfy conation, but the possession of these characteristics in relation to other similar beings; that is, it includes the awareness of others as having conations, and involves the satisfying, or the capacity to satisfy, their conations as well as our own.

Acts of specific obligation arising from love, friendship, or other association, plainly involve an inter-personal tie. Love or friendship is inter-personal, and the obligation of acts due to friendship is an expression, and a cementing, of that inter-personal union. The same is true of other forms of association, though the inter-personal union is usually less intense than that of love or friendship.

All acts of specific obligation therefore involve a metaphorical tie or bond. To think of oneself as having such an obligation to another person is to think of oneself as 'bound' to him in virtue of what has previously passed between us. What we are obliged to do, that which the bond requires of us, is in some specific way to promote the interests of the person to whom we are bound.

Can we say the same sort of thing about obligations of general incidence? What we are here obliged to do is again concerned with the promotion of the interests of those to whom we have obligations. Non-interference with the liberty of others is refraining from thwarting their own pursuit of their happiness, and so is, in a negative sense, co-operation with them in the promotion of their interests. To avoid paining others is similarly to refrain from thwarting their desires, for everyone normally desires to be free from pain. To relieve pain is a positive form of helping to satisfy this desire. Veracity is satisfying the desire to know.

The remaining principle of general obligation in our first classification is treatment on a basis of equality. This is concerned with the form rather than the content of our general obligations. In our second classification it is shown as characterizing all obligations of general incidence. It is a way of saying that these obligations are owed to all without discrimination, and in at least some of its manifestations it implies some positive sense in which all men are to be rated equally. We shall need to give special consideration to this point later. So far as the *content* of general obligations is concerned, they all have to do with the satisfying of the interests of others.

They do not depend, as do obligations of specific incidence, on the thought of what has passed between the person obliged and those to whom he is obliged. But they do depend on the possibility of knowing or believing that the person to whom the obligation is due has affective-conative dispositions to be satisfied. Consciousness of the interests of others, of them as conative beings like ourselves, and of our capacity to help satisfy those interests, is again the inter-personal relation of morality or moral personality. Men are able to be moral persons in virtue of the joint possession of three kinds of capacity. First, they are conscious of their own conative-affective tendencies; second, they can enter, in sympathetic imagination, into the similar experiences of others; and third, they can help each other to satisfy their interests. These capacities enable them to form a general policy of guiding their lives so as to respect and promote the ends of others as well as of themselves. It is thus that we become members of 'a realm of ends' or 'members of one another'.

It is not always necessary that the agent who has an obligation should actually be imagining the needs or wishes of those to whom he is obliged. But it is necessary that he should be capable of imagining them, if he is to be counted as a moral agent having obligations; and it is also necessary that *somebody* should be aware of the claimant's needs and desires, if we are to speak of there being any obligations towards him. Now the inter-personal relationship is a thinking of the interests of the person having the claim, and thinking of them as capable of being satisfied by the action or co-operation (positive or negative) of some other person or persons. Often, the thinking of the claimant's interests is done by the moral agent having the obligation. If someone asks me a question, it can normally be assumed that I understand that he desires the information. Sometimes this might not be true. If I am in a foreign country with a poor knowledge of the language, I may fail to realize that a remark addressed to me is a request for information. We should not then say that I have an obligation to give it until I realize that a request is being made. If I think, rightly or wrongly, that someone is in pain and I can help, I have an obligation to do so. But if I did not know that someone, whom I could help if I did know, were in distress, we should not normally say that I was under an obligation.

There are instances, however, where we should attribute obligations even though the agent having the obligation were not himself aware of the need to be satisfied. Consider the social claim of equal satisfactions up to a 'standard level'.

Schemes of social security and social welfare try to make provision for this. In contributing to social insurance funds, and in paying rates and taxes part of which will be used, say, for communal education, I am not necessarily, and certainly not merely, joining in a scheme of mutual *self*-help. I may or may not expect to receive security for myself against unemployment or sickness. I may or may not expect for my family, if I have one, a share in the communal education service. These schemes rest on the idea that all the members of the community stand in together and are, literally and in everyday action, responsible for one another's needs. If I have no fear of unemployment or no need of national sickness benefit, if I have no children to be educated or if I choose to pay additionally for them to be educated privately, I still have a moral (as well as a legal) obligation to contribute to the common funds in order that other members of the community, who do need these services, may have them. Now I obviously cannot know about all the individuals who have these needs; and if I have never seen the effects of unemployment I may not have even a general idea of the kind of need that the unemployment fund serves. But the scheme would not have come into existence unless some people (other than those who have the need) had been conscious of the evils of unemployment and the possibility of lightening these evils by social action. And when the scheme is in existence, somebody must know about Tom Jones's unemployment before the state, acting on behalf of the community, can have an obligation to help him.

Obligations of this kind depend on a general sentiment of society. They might be called obligations of social morality as distinguished from obligations of individual morality. Since I am holding that obligations are always to other persons, both types of obligation might be called, in a sense, social, the 'society' involved in the second type being formed by the sense of community between the persons involved in the tie. The distinction between the two is that, in the second type there is a definite inter-personal relation between the person obliged and the claimant, while in the first the obligation rests upon a general sense of responsibility held to apply to all members of a group even though they may not individually be involved in an inter-personal relation with each other. The obligations which I am calling social arise from the needs of the persons said to have claims, together with the general sense of community that makes the class of persons involved a 'society'. With such obligations, the inter-personal relation is held, by a kind of moral fiction (analogous to a legal fiction) to characterize all adult members of the society, even though an obliged person may not in fact have the awareness of the needs, desires, or expectations, of another, which normally constitutes that relationship. What I want to suggest is that the experience of sympathetically imagining the conative-affective experiences of others gives rise to the idea of inter-personal relationship, and then that idea may be applied, by a fiction, to situations in which the experience is not present.

The sympathetic imagination of the wishes of others is not always held to involve an obligation. It is so far as negative action is concerned. If there are no countervailing ethical considerations, there is always an obligation not to thwart the desires of others. But positive action to satisfy the desires of others is sometimes obligatory, sometimes merely fitting. The claims of justice and friendship, as set out in our second classification, summarize a range of interests, within which action to serve the ends of others is obligatory. Beyond that range, action to promote the positive good of others is, for the average moral agent, fitting but not obligatory. For instance, the removal of pain, where we can, is obligatory towards all and sundry; but not, generally speaking, the addition of positive pleasure. The latter is obligatory in the special circumstances of a good many claims of specific incidence, notably the claims of gratitude, merit, and association (love, friendship, kinship, and so forth). The positive satisfaction of interests is also generally obligatory within a community up to what is regarded as the 'standard level'. This is seen in the claims of equal opportunity and of equal satisfaction of basic needs. The extent of the 'community', in which some such positive general obligations will be recognized, varies. Most people will think that they have definite obligations of this sort to the members of their state. They may or may not think that their obligation to the members of their city is higher. They may or may not think that they have similar obligations, though to a lesser degree (some would say to the same degree), towards the members of communities beyond the national, e.g. to all the members of the human race.

Roughly speaking, then, the claims of justice and friendship set the bounds of the obligatory as opposed to the merely fitting. These bounds are not fixed for all time. They differ at different times and places. The shifting of the bounds may be due to economic necessity or to the widening or narrowing of men's moral horizon. Even at one time and place, particular individuals are likely to have a wider moral horizon than others. What is supererogation for the average man may be regarded as obligatory by a few. One of the functions of the concept of justice, especially in the sphere of social obligation, is to conserve and consolidate the level of morality generally regarded as obligatory, to insist upon accepted rights, leaving it to individuals to go beyond that range of beneficent action, to be generous as well as just, thus setting an example for a raising of the level generally regarded as socially obligatory.

§3. *The nature of fittingness and goodness*

Beyond the level of the obligatory is the sphere of fitting or good action that is not (at any rate yet) generally regarded as obligatory. But all right action is at least fitting, i.e. a means to the promotion of good or the diminution of evil. This includes, as obligatory action does not, the promotion of one's own good. Acts commonly regarded as obligatory are therefore distinguished from fitting acts (*a*) by involving a real or fictitious inter-personal relation, and (*b*) by being included in the range of justice and friendship. Are these the sole differences? In setting out the second classification of right acts, I said that all right acts are intended to produce good or to remove, and refrain from producing, evil. But in speaking of obligatory acts I have said that their content always relates to the *interests* of other persons or creatures. Does this imply that I regard good and evil as always concerned with interests? The answer is yes.

By 'interests' I mean enjoyments and objects of desire. The existence of both is due to the fact that men (and certain other creatures) have conative-affective dispositions. Fittingness depends on the existence of conative tendencies and their aiming at satisfaction. Obligation depends on this together with the idea of inter-personal ties. We have equated a fitting act with an act that aims at good or at the removal or prevention of evil. For convenience, we may use the expression 'aims at good' to cover the removal and prevention of evil also. My account then implies that goodness (other than moral goodness, which we have defined in terms of duty) always relates to the satisfaction of interests; that a fitting or instrumentally good act is always one that aims at someone's good (i.e. someone's interest); that, indeed, the fittingness of such an act simply derives from the fact that it is directed to the realizing of someone's interest; and that the goodness of a state of affairs derives from the fact that such a state of affairs is someone's good. I am, in effect, taking what is called a naturalistic view of fittingness or goodness, for I am saying that so-called intrinsic goodness, other than moral goodness, is, in the end, called good simply because it is, or serves, someone's good, i.e. someone's interest.[1]

There is, it seems to me, a grain of truth in Hobbes's view that what is called good (other than morally good—even Hobbes gave a different, though unacceptable, account of the 'worth' of persons) is the object of desire. But Hobbes was mistaken in making the definition egoistic by restricting a man's use of the word 'good' to what satisfies *his own* desire. Most

[1]The view outlined here has affinities with the position of Professor C. A. Campbell in his paper 'Moral and Non-Moral Values', *Mind,* July, 1935. This is criticized by Sir David Ross in *Foundations of Ethics*, pp. 262-71, the crucial issue being presented on pp. 266-7. For my own doubts about naturalism and intuitionism alike, see ch. ix, §2, below.

agathists have agreed that non-instrumental goods are always states of mind. If we look at their lists of good states of mind, we shall find that these are all states which satisfy conative tendencies. The usual list is happiness (or pleasure), virtue (i.e. moral goodness and what we are calling excellences of character), knowledge, and the creation and appreciation of beauty. I should be inclined to say that the word 'happiness' just is a vague way of referring summarily to all that one wants for oneself. But if we take the alternative word 'pleasure', which figures in some formulations of the list of intrinsic goods, pleasure is the feeling tone that accompanies or colours the satisfaction of desire, and is itself occasionally a direct object of desire. Knowledge is useful for the promotion of happiness and satisfies the desire of curiosity. The appreciation of beauty is a form of pleasure and perhaps of rational insight. The creation of beauty gives pleasure and satisfies the creative urge. As to virtue, we have left out of the account one type of virtue, that which we are calling moral goodness. Excellences of character, or dispositional virtues, are both useful and aesthetically pleasing. I think that the account of virtue given by Hutcheson and Hume is substantially correct for excellences of character, which is what they were talking about, under the name of 'benevolence'; they did not discuss moral goodness as something different from benevolence, and that omission is what wrecks their account if taken, as they evidently intended it, to cover all virtue. But I agree with them in thinking that the goodness of 'benevolence' or 'natural' virtue lies in its utility (i.e. in its being usually a means to other goods) and in its being attractive, lovable, in the kind of way, though not in precisely the same way, that beauty is attractive.

Although this view of fittingness or goodness is in a sense naturalistic, it should be noted that I am not committing what Professor Moore called the naturalistic fallacy, that is, I am not saying that 'good' always *means* 'what satisfies desire'. I am not saying that the word 'good', as used in normative judgements of ordinary life, can be replaced, without loss or addition of connotation, by 'naturalistic' or non-normative terms. Part of its connotation consists in its syntactical relations within the system of ethical language, and I have agreed, in discussing the logic of moral concepts, that those uses of 'good' which are felt to be specifically normative uses can be replaced only by other specifically normative terms, such as 'fitting'. But I agree with the naturalists that the entity to which the word 'good' ultimately refers is interest.

Then how do some uses of 'good' in ordinary discourse come to be thought of as specifically 'ethical' or 'normative'? A 'positive' use of the word simply states a matter of fact. 'My good' is my interest, the object of those of my natural desires that are directed towards future states of myself; 'the good of all' is the interest of all. The word 'fitting' also may be used in a positive sense. What causes or is a successful means to a proposed end, an object of desire, is 'fitting' or 'suitable' for the realization of that end. Such an end may be, *ethically*, good or bad. Since it is an object of desire it is, *pro tanto,* necessarily 'good' in the positive sense of that word; this proposition is a tautology. If its realization involves thwarting other ends (of the same person or of other persons), then such thwarting is, *pro tanto,* 'bad'. An act which realizes the one end and thwarts the others is, in relation to the successful realization of one 'good', a 'fitting' act; in relation to the thwarting of other 'goods', i.e., since it realizes 'evils', it is an 'unfitting' act. If the total effect of the act is judged to contain more 'good' than 'evil', then the act is judged, on balance, to be 'fitting', i.e., it produces more good than harm. All these uses of the words 'good', evil', and 'fitting', are positive. They simply—or rather, mainly—describe what are taken to be facts, and the facts so described are 'natural' facts.

A 'normative' use of a word connotes, in addition, a stimulus to action; it has an evocative or imperative force. I do not wish to deny that *any* use of 'good' or 'fitting' may have some evocative force. If I describe the object of my natural desires as my 'good', there may be some evocative force in the expression. Words rarely have *only* a descriptive force. But since egoistic desires are so strong in all of us, a reference to my own interest does not usually need the interpolation of a stimulus to dispose me to pursue it. It can be taken for granted that I am so disposed already, and the non-descriptive force of 'my good' is more *expressive* of my already existing disposition than evocative, though the expression of my own disposition may carry a prohibitory hint to others against interference. The non-descriptive force of 'my good' might be evocative to myself also, if my disposition to pursue my happiness on the whole is inhibited by some urgent desire to pursue a particular end that I can see will militate against my interest on the whole. Then the reference to my interest as 'my good' no longer expresses the force of a felt desire so much as it recalls former expressions of the desire; and the effect of this is to evoke the desire, to stimulate a manifestation of the disposition. In so far as 'good', used with a reference to one's own interest, has such an evocative force, it is normative or at least quasi-normative.

The evocative stimulus is, however, more common in reference to disinterested ends of action. Disinterested desires have, for most people at most times, a much weaker force than self-interest. Accordingly a reference to disinterested ends, if it is intended to provoke action or a readiness to act, often needs a stimulus, and this is given in the evocative force of the words used, thereby causing them to be used 'normatively'. To say that if people desire happiness, then happiness as such is *a* good (as opposed to being *their* good) or is 'in itself' a fitting object of pursuit, is to pass from a description of the natural tendency of each man to pursue his own happiness, to an evocation of a readiness to promote happiness no matter whose. I do not mean that there are no pre-existing disinterested desires. If men had no vestige of disinterested feelings or desires, it would be quite useless to try to stir them up by 'normative' language; there would be nothing to be stimulated. Often there is no need for the stimulus of normative language to cause a man to act disinterestedly. Often, too, there is need for a stimulus to cause him to follow his own interest on the whole.

The evocative or 'imperative' force of normative words is

not just the same as the force of any imperative form of language. A command is often limited to a particular occasion, expressing a short-lived desire and referring to an individual action. Normative words express a general policy to be followed in all situations of a similar kind. If a Minister of the Crown says in a public speech, 'we must increase productivity', he is urging his direct and indirect audience to follow a course of action. But what he is urging them to do is not confined to a particular action on the day of his speech, and what he is expressing is not a desire that he happens to feel just then. His statement is an expression of a general policy to be applied over a period in a variety of situations, a policy the force of which he and his colleagues expect to feel for some time. Ethical imperatives express policies of action recommended for all persons and for all relevant occasions. To say that happiness is a good or a fitting object of pursuit is implicitly to recommend to anyone the pursuit of such happiness, no matter whose, as can be pursued at any time. What is referred to by 'good' is a 'natural' entity, but the normative force of the word cannot be given a simple naturalistic interpretation as issuing from the contingent desires of the person using the word. The imperative force is a 'demand of reason', i.e. a prescription of universal application. Like legal judgements, moral judgements depend upon 'commands' that are universally legislative.

A general policy of action may prescribe a means to an already accepted end. 'We must increase productivity' prescribes a means to increasing the general standard of living, or to maintaining the existing standard. Most legal Statutes are similarly 'hypothetical imperatives'. Alternatively, however, a general policy may prescribe an end to be adopted. Those principles of Common Law that lawyers call principles of 'Natural Justice' are, unlike Statutes, of this nature, and so are ethical policies. ('Natural Justice' is simply a name for certain generally accepted principles of ethics.) 'The happiness of all is a fitting object of pursuit' prescribes an end. The adoption of an end is prescribed only where it would not automatically come about, and therefore it can always be challenged. If there are alternative policies that may be adopted, we may ask why we should adopt this one rather than an alternative. An 'imperative' theory of normative language, therefore, does not dispose of the old question, why should I accept the prescriptions of morality? The question, 'Why ought I to do my duty?' is a pseudo-question if it means 'Why ought I to do what I ought to do?' If I allow that something is what I ought to do, I have agreed that I ought to do it. But to ask, 'Why should I accept this rather than that as my policy of action?' is to pose a genuine question. An imperative theory of normative language still leaves us with 'ultimate norms'. The normative force of the statement 'It is fitting to pursue the interests of all' may be explained as expressing and recommending a general policy of action, but this does not dispose of all problems about normative judgements. It simply shows the difference between the positive (or descriptive) and the normative use of words like 'fitting' and 'good'.

There is an obvious objection to the view that the denotative reference of the ethical uses of 'fitting' or 'good' is the same as that of their positive uses. We do not think it fitting to satisfy *all* desires. Some desires and conative potentialities, it may be said, are bad, things which it is fitting to repress, not to satisfy and nurture.

I do not think this difficulty need detain us long. The satisfaction of any conation is, as being such, fitting or good. If the satisfaction of it does not involve the thwarting or stifling of others, felt more strongly and more widely, in the individual himself or in other persons, we continue to call it good. If, however, it does involve the thwarting of other interests, it is in that respect instrumentally bad or unfitting; and if the conations whose satisfaction it will thwart are more strongly or more widely felt than the one which will be satisfied, then the satisfaction of that one conation is, on balance, bad, i.e., it involves the thwarting of interests more than their satisfaction. Since it is on balance fitting to satisfy the other interests, to which the original one is opposed, it is derivatively fitting to take action which will lead to the satisfaction, or prevent the non-satisfaction, of the predominant set of interests, and therefore it is fitting to suppress the original interest. Although the satisfaction of the 'bad' tendency is, considered merely as the satisfaction of an interest, *pro tanto* fitting, that fittingness is outweighed by the greater fittingness of satisfying the others which it would thwart. This talk of one fittingness outweighing another is only a way of saying that the satisfaction of the second set of interests is more strongly or more widely desired. Desirability *is* after all a function of being desired, though not of being desired *simpliciter* but of being desired with reference to the whole system of desires and potential desires of an individual and of the community of persons. So far as the system of the desires of the individual is concerned, this is just a form of the harmony doctrine urged from Plato onwards. My desire to get drunk should be discouraged (even where it is unlikely to cause me to neglect obligations), because it is likely to prevent me from satisfying other interests which I should prefer if I reflected on what I wanted most and taking into account my whole life. I should say, however, that when confined to the individual, such 'desirability' has a normative but not a moral connotation. It has a moral connotation when it takes in the desires of others.

§4. *The nature of moral obligation*

I have argued that the rightness of fitting acts, no less than of obligatory acts, lies in their realizing the interests of persons (and other conative-affective creatures). There is no good that is not, ultimately, either identical with, or dependent upon, the good (i.e. the interest) *of* someone. I have also argued that moral obligations are always altruistic. The pursuit of my own interest may be normatively as well as positively fitting, but it is not obligatory. An obligation is thought of as a tie to some other person or persons, and refers to the pursuit of ἀλλότριον ἀγαθόν in conditions where that is thought to be not only fitting but more forcefully demanded.

The normative use of the word 'ought' carries a stronger evocative or imperative force than that attaching to the normative use of 'good' or 'fitting'. This imperative force of 'ought' is not confined to moral obligation. The so-called hypothetical sense of 'ought' connotes a requirement or imperative no less than the moral or so-called categorical sense. The two senses differ, however, in their objects of reference. The hypothetical 'ought' refers to a causal relation of means and ends. The idea of moral obligation also arises from reference to an entity existing in the world. The 'entity' in this case is the thought of an inter-personal tie, an imaginative act of regarding oneself as related to another person's ends (i.e. his interests) in the way in which one naturally regards oneself as related to one's own ends, that is, as disposed to pursue them. But because the imaginative act does not involve the delusion of thinking that I *am* the other person whose ends I propose to pursue, nor of thinking that I *am* disposed to pursue his ends, the proposed pursuit is called an 'obligation' as opposed to the natural 'desire' which we should feel towards our own ends and which we sometimes do feel towards the ends of others.

Like my account of fittingness or good, this account of moral obligation may be called 'naturalistic', since the original object of reference giving rise to the idea of obligation is something that exists in the world of nature. It is not, however, a 'natural' feeling or desire such as most naturalists wish to use as the kind of object referred to by all ethical words, but is a thought or imaginative act; Moore, I think (at least judging by the doctrines of *Principia Ethica*), would call it a 'natural' entity. But both with 'fitting' or 'good' (in their normative uses) and with 'obligation' I do not give a naturalistic *definition*, i.e. a substitutable expression for the occurrence of these words in ethical language. Such definitions must keep within the fence of ethical language, and are dealt with in the logic of morals.

Let us consider a little more precisely what this account of moral obligation comes to. The sympathetic representation in imagination of another's interests which we can help satisfy gives rise to the idea of an inter-personal tie. We think of ourselves as bound to the person whose ends we represent to ourselves, we think of his ends as if they were our own (in which case we should naturally pursue them), while yet being conscious that they are in fact the ends of another person and not of ourselves, so that the natural desire to pursue the ends contemplated is not necessarily evoked. To think that we *ought* to pursue his ends is to strive to feel towards his ends as we should naturally feel towards our own. The conation thus evoked is what is referred to by the idea of moral obligation. To *say* that I am obliged is not to say that I *have* this conation. Still more obviously, to say to or of another man that he is obliged is not to say that he *has* the conation. Once the *idea* of a (metaphorical) bond to another person has arisen, it has its own meaning of, simply, a bond or requirement. We assert its presence in circumstances where, we think, a 'moral person', that is, a man who follows a general policy of treating the ends of others as his own, would *feel* the 'tie'.

Our capacity to serve the interests of others, however, is limited, both because of the strength of egoistic desires which may conflict with the thought of altruistic action, and because my serving the interests of *A* will often prevent my serving the interests of *B*. Therefore implicit conventions have arisen that only in certain types of situation is altruistic action strictly obligatory as opposed to fitting, and that in such-and-such a set of circumstances my obligation to *A* is greater than my obligation to *B*. These conventions are usually due to the relative strength of most people's natural dispositions or to proved social utility, and often to a combination of both. Most people are more ready to imagine, sympathize with, and help satisfy, the interests of their close familiars, such as kin and friends, than of comparative strangers. Consequently, a general convention to the effect that, e.g., parents should take special responsibility for looking after their children, is found to be a practicable means of achieving for most children the care they need. But further experience or changes in social circumstances may alter traditional views, as when it is found that certain forms of education can be more successfully given by communal effort. Even the original convention owes something to utility, for it achieves more than the natural disposition of most parents would achieve by itself. The convention canalizes the disposition and tends, by the force of example and general approbation, to check the fecklessness which some parents would otherwise show. It might be argued, from anthropological evidence, that some of the allegedly 'natural' or 'instinctive' tendencies have themselves been nurtured by the growth of social custom. The different histories and environments of different societies cause different conventions to be adopted, or different emphases to be placed on similar conventions; obligations to family were stronger in traditional Chinese society than in the west; the obligations of hospitality to any passing stranger were stronger in ancient Greece than they are in modern Europe. At any rate, it has been found useful to direct responsibility along fairly narrow channels, lest diffusion rob the stream of adequate force. Particular types of situation in which one person can make the ends of others his own, are singled out, by the growth of convention, as *specifically* obligatory on particular groups of persons.

Among these specific principles of obligation, promises and contracts hold a peculiar place. The mere utterance of a certain form of words is held to give rise, of itself, to a specific bond. To promise, to say 'I undertake' or 'I promise you' or (emphatically) 'I will do so-and-so', is itself to bind oneself to act as one says one will. There is, as it were, a pre-existing understanding that the use of such a form of words between two men binds them by a specific inter-personal tie like that which is held to obtain, and which often would obtain without the force of convention, between kinsmen, friends, benefactor and beneficiary, etc. The understanding regarding promises and contracts is presumably also a convention that has grown up through proved utility. It is peculiar in that the 'moral fiction' here is one whereby 'mere words and breath' are themselves held to make the bond.

I have spoken of the 'tie' of moral obligation as an inter-personal relation. The name is suitable enough when the parties at each side of the tie are mutually capable of that sympathetic imagination which helps to make us persons. But the whole of this condition is not necessary for there to be an obligation. What I am calling the 'inter-personal relation' is, strictly speaking, an imaginative experience in the mind of *one* person. I call it a *relation* to another person because the imaginative act has as its object the supposed experience of another. As I pointed out in §1, however, the object of the moral agent's thought need not be another rational agent; it is enough that the being of whom the moral agent thinks should have conations and affections. The 'inter-personal relation' may be directed towards animals as well as human beings. But we do not regard animals as persons, and the name, 'inter-personal' relation, may be misleading in its suggestion that the claimant as well as the agent must always be a 'person'. Animals are not able to enter with us into reciprocal relations of sympathetic understanding, not having our imaginative capacities. But we think of them as having conations, e.g. for the avoidance of pain and perhaps to some extent for getting pleasure. At any rate we assume that they enjoy pleasure and dislike pain, though perhaps we should not say they 'desire' to get the one and avoid the other, since this would involve imaginative prospection of these feelings. But they have 'interests', namely satisfactions and objects of conative urges. If we choose, we may say that animals partake of an element of personality to the extent of having interests. But since personality is communal and depends on (or rather, is in part) the capacity for mutual sympathetic understanding, we do not normally say that animals are persons.

In so far as there can be community between men and animals (e.g. between a man and his dog, conscious of each other as beings with interests, and fond of each other), we can perhaps say that an animal may become a person. The supposition that a dog may have for his master in some degree the sort of sympathy that another man could have, is perhaps an illusion; but the dog-lover who does imagine this, does regard his dog as a person in its own right. All our use of moral language depends on what we fallibly take to be facts. We may be quite wrong in thinking that animals generally have little or no reason or imagination, or that plants are not literally sensitive. If we thought that such qualities were possessed by animals and plants, we should extend the use of our moral language and alter our attitudes and conduct towards them. The inter-personal relation of which I am speaking has some affinities with the relation between persons described by Martin Buber in his book *I and Thou*—though I think he regards the awareness of another person as a form of direct knowledge and not as a sympathetic representation of the imagination. In order to illustrate the relation, he recounts[1] an experience, which he has met several times, of confronting a cat and finding the cat conscious of his regarding it as a person able to enter into the 'I-thou' relationship. Most of us may feel that this is a flight of poetic imagination, like the literal ascription of sensitivity to a plant. But the point for our present purpose is, that if we regarded cats and dogs in this way, we should think of them as persons. We know by direct observation only the publicly observable behaviour (including the speech) of men, as of animals, and our awareness of their states of mind is imagination, which may be mistaken in either case. Our moral language and attitudes reflect the way in which we imagine the internal experience of others and think of our relation to it and its relation to us.

In speaking of the state of mind that gives rise to the idea of moral obligation, I have concentrated on its cognitive and conative aspects, imaginative understanding and the effort to pursue another's ends as if they were our own. But it can also be described by its affective characteristics. Awareness of someone as a person, and readiness to satisfy his interests, go along with affective experiences, which have been considered by some moralists to constitute the whole of the state of mind called sympathy or benevolence. Affection (i.e. in the everyday, not the wider psychological, sense), or love proper, as op-

[1] English translation, p. 97.

posed to mere physical attraction or to aesthetic admiration, always, I think, includes cognition of the 'I-thou' type, i.e. of the object of love as a person to whom one is inter-personally related. Hence the view frequently expressed (e.g. in Spinoza and McTaggart) that perfect knowledge (knowledge of a person, that is) is the same as perfect love. Here too we find the union of the ethics of obligation with the ethics of love. 'Love thy neighbour as thyself' is an injunction to feel towards our neighbour's ends as we should naturally feel towards our own. Most men are capable of loving their wives and children as themselves, so as to act naturally towards them as moral obligation would require. But it is not psychologically possible, save perhaps for a few rare souls, that a man should feel thus towards all his 'neighbours', i.e. towards anyone whom he can affect by his actions, if only because he cannot have for all his neighbours that measure of sympathetic understanding which is necessary for love and which he may have for close familiars. Accordingly the idea of moral obligation expresses an injunction, a stimulus, at least to *act* towards our neighbours as we should naturally act if we loved them as ourselves, and as we do all naturally act towards ourselves through the strength of self-love. The legislative prescriptions of *Leviticus* are summed up in its maxim of love;[1] and both Jesus of Nazareth and his older contemporary Hillel, accepting 'thou shalt love thy neighbour as thyself' as the sum of Old Testament ethics, interpreted it, by the 'Golden Rule', in terms of *action* towards all men. The writer of the Pentateuch also knew *how* it is possible to 'love as thyself' the neighbour who is not literally among our loved ones. The well known chapter of *Leviticus* that tells us to love our neighbour as ourselves goes on to explain that this includes the stranger: 'and thou shalt love him as thyself; for ye were strangers in the land of Egypt'.[2] The point of the ground assigned here for obligations to strangers is expanded in *Exodus*:[3] 'for ye *know the heart* of a stranger, seeing ye were strangers in the land of Egypt'. It is because we take others to have like experiences to our own

[1]Ch. xix, v. 18. [2]Ibid., v. 34. [3]Ch. xxiii, v. 9.

that we can feel for them the sympathetic understanding which is a condition of love and of moral obligation alike.

Some of Kant's remarks concerning the Categorical Imperative may be regarded as giving succinctly the view of moral obligation that I am suggesting, though it is necessary to add that Kant's *dominant* interpretation of the Categorical Imperative, even in the formulae of 'ends-in-themselves', is not the one that I am stressing at this point. In his formulations of the Categorical Imperative in terms of ends, Kant says that we are to treat persons as ends, which means, he says, that we are to make their ends our own, i.e., join with them in satisfying their purposes. In doing this we act as persons, members of one another or of a 'realm of ends'. Because Kant tries to unify obligations in this way, I should not class him with those deontologists who leave us with an 'unconnected heap' of obligations. My suggestion is that Kant's formulations of the Categorical Imperative in terms of ends, as here interpreted, constitute the unifying principle presupposed by the logic of morals. The later deontologists have given us an account of the logic of morals. Kant has given us the metaphysic of morals.

§5. *Equality and ends-in-themselves*

In §2 we ran through the various principles of obligation to see what was the idea of obligation common to them all. We left aside for separate consideration the principle of treating on a basis of equality all those whom we may affect by our action. The claim of equality, I said, relates to the form, rather than the content, of all obligations of general incidence. The hedonistic utilitarians were right to separate the principle of equality from the ends aimed at by right action.

Our second classification of right acts set out three claims of distributive justice, three applications of the formal principle of equal treatment: (1) the claim of equal liberty, (2) the claim of equal opportunity, and (3) the claim of equal satisfactions up to a conventionally accepted, minimum level. The claim of equal liberty asserts that the private ends of every individual are to be respected. Each individual is to count equally. In Chapter V, I argued that the other two claims of distributive justice, which require positive action on the part of other people towards those who have the claims, likewise depend on valuing individuals as such. The claim of equal opportunity, however, involves considerations of utility also. We think that self-development is due to each person as an 'end-in-himself', but the development of many human capacities is also useful to society at large, though in different degrees. 'Equal opportunity' means opportunity for all, but differentiated according to their different capacities. To say that all men have a claim to equality is not to say that they are equal in capacity or 'worth'; but it is to say, in some sense, that they are to be regarded as of equal value.

We regard human beings as in one sense of equal value, in another not. If we think of economic or instrumental value, i.e. utility, they are unequal. If we think of them as 'ends-in-themselves', they are not unequal. Why is this? To speak of differences in value, other than instrumental value, as between different people, is something of a paradox. A chattel or an animal is said to be valuable when we mean that it is useful for satisfying the needs and desires of men. In so far as men are useful to each other, their (instrumental) value can be rated. But when we think of them as 'ends', not as means, we are thinking of them as that for the sake of which means are counted instrumentally valuable; i.e., we regard *their* ends, their purposes, the satisfaction of their desires, as that for the sake of which other things are valued. One function of the statement that men are not simply means to further ends but are ends in themselves, is to draw attention to the fact that the satisfaction of human interests is that for the sake of which other things (and often men themselves in reference to their useful capacities and dispositions) are said to have relative or instrumental value. Consequently, the 'value' of human beings as ends cannot be rated on the same scale as the value of things (including human capacities and dispositions) that are valued as means and that can be rated relatively to one another. Value as an end is not commensurable with instrumental values.[1] We are prepared to rate one kind of human end against another, since a person may organize his ends into a hierarchy, choosing some in preference to others. But we are not prepared to rate against each other the persons who have the ends or make the choices.

With regard to animals our attitude is ambivalent. In thinking that we have some obligation to respect their affections and conations, we are thinking of their ends as ends. But when we rate things, including animals and men, as having instrumental value, we do not usually include the ends of animals among the ends that constitute our standard of reference, means to which are to be counted as instrumentally valuable. We think only of human ends. Where human ends conflict with animal ends, most of us have little compunction in treating animals simply as means to human ends. But if the ends of one human being conflict with the ends of another, we think that both are to be taken into account as 'ends-in-themselves'. Hence we say that all men have equal claims to our consideration, that they are all equally ends-in-themselves.

The above account of the equality of men as ends-in-themselves owes much to Professor W. T. Stace's stimulating book *The Destiny of Western Man*. But Professor Stace gives it as an interpretation of the Christian doctrine of 'the infinite value' of the individual or of the human soul. I think that the doctrine of the *infinite* value or worth of men relates to their potentiality for *moral* worth. The Stoics said that in virtue (what we are calling moral goodness) a man may equal the gods; for to be perfectly moral is to do right to the utmost of one's capacity. An infinite being, with infinite capacity, can do infinite good. A finite being, with finite capacity, cannot do more good than his capacity allows. Hence, if he does good intentionally to the limits of his capacity, he is perfectly moral. In this one respect a man may achieve perfection, he may be of as much moral worth as an infinite being. Obviously a poor

[1]Cf. W. T. Stace, *The Destiny of Western Man*, ch. vi.

and ignorant man may be as morally worthy as a rich and wise man, though he cannot do as much good. In the same way, the Stoics taught, a man can be as morally worthy as a god if he acts up to the limit of his capacity for doing good. In respect of moral goodness, men have the capacity to equal the gods, to reach perfection of infinity. I think that 'the infinite worth' of man refers to his potentiality for reaching perfection, for imitating the perfection or infinity of God, in this one respect. The phrase refers, like 'the dignity of man', to the human capacity for moral agency.

Now when Kant says that men are ends-in-themselves, he sometimes appears to have in mind the second of these conceptions, and sometimes the first. When he says that men are ends-in-themselves in virtue of being autonomous, of legislating for themselves, of being the authors of their morality, he thinks of them as moral *agents*. Accordingly, when he tells us that we should treat them as ends-in-themselves, he seems to mean that we should think of them as moral agents, like ourselves, forming moral conceptions that are universally legislative for all men. But elsewhere he says that to treat men as ends implies that we should make their ends our own, and this would seem to be thinking of them as having, like ourselves, interests or ends for the sake of which actions are done. Again, Kant says that we owe to others the promotion of their happiness, and to ourselves the promotion of our perfection or virtue. This suggests that in thinking of other people as affected by our action, to regard them as ends is to think of them as conative beings whose purposes we should try to satisfy; while in thinking of ourselves as the performers of actions, to regard ourselves as ends is to think of ourselves as moral agents. The two conceptions could be joined together by including in 'the ends' of others not only their natural ends or interests, but also their moral ends or universally legislative policies—assuming, as Kant optimistically does assume, that the consciences of all men coincide in their general moral policy. This would imply that, as moral agents, we should adopt as our ends the natural ends of others, i.e., that we should try to serve their interests, and that we should also accept, as identical with our moral policy binding upon us, the moral end that they prescribe in their moral judgements. The two kinds of end adopted by the moral agent are not in fact separate ends. The first represents the content of the policy adopted, the second represents its form as a universal 'law' emanating from all moral agents and binding upon all moral agents.

These suggestions are not based on any close study of Kant, and I dare say that they are wide of the mark if taken as an interpretation of Kant's doctrine. But it seems to me that the conclusion I have drawn from him is the right one for moral theory. To think of others as persons, as entering into moral relationship with us, is to think of two different things; first, it is to think of them as having interests and of the possibility of our helping to satisfy those interests; secondly, it is to think of them as moral agents whose judgements we should respect as laying down the moral law not only for themselves but for everyone. To think of ourselves as persons, as entering into moral relationship with others, is to think of ourselves, not as having interests (self-love will look after that), but as moral agents able to serve the interests of others and as subject to a moral law that is universally applicable and universally made by moral agents in a 'realm of ends'. As moral agents we must 'legislate' for ourselves, but as moral subjects of a 'realm of ends' we must take heed of, and are at least to some extent bound by, the 'legislation' of the community of moral agents. We have no prerogative of moral judgement; in that respect, too, all men are equal.

§6. *Subjective and objective duty*

To be a moral agent, to be capable of having obligations, a person must be capable of sympathetically imagining the interests of others. But it is not true that in order to have a particular obligation a man must have a sympathetic understanding of the facts which give rise to his obligation. We may say of a callous parent that he ought not to neglect his child, even though we may think he has no sympathetic feelings for the child's misery. The parent himself might think he has an obligation even though he has no affection for the child, simply because he accepts the generally held principle that parents have special obligations to their children. For some obligations, sympathy seems quite out of place; if I acknowledge my obligation to pay a creditor I am not thereby shedding silent tears for his needs. I may even have an obligation without being aware of it, as when I forget that I have made a promise. The view we have put forward is that the *idea* of moral obligation, of an inter-personal tie, *arises* from sympathetic imagination of another's interests which we can help promote; but once the idea has arisen, it is applied, by convention, to certain stock types of situation in which there may not actually be, on the part of the agent, consciousness of the interest which he is obliged to promote.

There is involved here the tangled question whether obligation and duty depend on the morally relevant facts of the situation, or on the agent's knowledge of or belief about those facts. And if the second alternative is adopted, there arises the additional question whether the agent's duty depends on what he judges to be the act morally called for by the situation as he sees it, or on what *is* the act morally called for by the situation as he sees it.

I do not think that common-sense moral judgements allow us to give a single answer, in favour of the 'objective' or in favour of the 'subjective' view, to cover all instances. Very often we say that a man ought to follow his own conscience, for he can (morally speaking) do no other. At times, however, it seems to me, we are ready not merely to say that a man's conscience is mistaken but to insist that his duty, what he ought to have done, lay in a different direction.

Taking the first question first; I am inclined to say that certain kinds of obligation, those which I have earlier distinguished as 'obligations of social morality', need not depend on the agent's thought about the situation but may depend on the generally accepted thought about the situation. The latter phrase is my version of the objective view. I do not think that any moral obligation can arise without thought on the part of somebody, and I am suggesting that the so-called objective view should be re-interpreted so as to state that the obligation arises, not from any completely 'objective' facts, i.e. facts which need not be cognized by anyone, but from the thoughts of society, i.e. of most people in the society concerned. Thus legal obligations involve also a moral obligation to obey the law, because the commands of the law usually represent part of what society generally has deemed to be obligatory. (If a man thinks he ought to disobey the law for conscientious reasons, this does not mean that he has *no* moral obligation to obey the law, but that his obligation to obey the law is, in his judgement, outweighed by some conflicting obligation. The question whether the subjective or the objective view is to be accepted for the determination of duty in situations where obligations conflict, is, in my view, a matter that concerns the second kind of subjectivity, to be discussed shortly.) A man is obliged, morally as well as legally, to fulfil a contract he has made, even though he may have forgotten it; to contribute to social security funds even though he may be unaware of the needs that these funds are to relieve. Obligations of social morality extend beyond the province of law, however. A man is morally and legally obliged to avoid cruelty to his children; but he is also morally, though not legally, obliged to give them such measure of care as most people in his society would regard as called for, even though he himself may (in some cases) not have the sympathetic consciousness of the children's needs that would make a *feeling* of obligation. For most parents, of course, this obligation is one of individual morality as well; i.e., they have an actual feeling of obligation to their children, in addition to realizing that society expects them to act as if they had. Any obligation of social morality may also be one of individual morality. Indeed it must be so for *some* moral agents; otherwise the kind of act concerned could not have become a generally accepted obligation. My point is that where a particular individual is not himself conscious of the relevant facts that give rise to the obligation, he is still obliged if the type of obligatory act in question is one that has been generally accepted as an obligation of social morality.

The 'society' whose general opinion determines which obligations are to fall within this category, varies in its extent with different obligations. With legal obligations, it is plainly the national community (as represented by the state), and in some instances the international community. With moral obligations, it may be the national community, or a smaller one, or a wider one. Some obligations of social morality apply, as irreducible demands of a community upon all its members, only to a small group; others to 'the civilized world' or to the whole of mankind. What is 'unprofessional conduct' in an English lawyer might not be regarded as a breach of obligation in an English layman. A list of 'human rights' attempts to set out the claims of all men (and so the obligations towards all men) that are generally accepted by the majority of mankind or the civilized world.

On the other hand, such obligations as do not come within the range of what is demanded by a society from all its members as an irreducible minimum, depend solely on what the agent thinks is required of him. A conscientious man will not regard his duties as confined within the range of what is absolutely demanded by society, but will think of that as merely a minimum required of even the morally weakest members of the community. A conscientious parent will think his duty to his child goes much farther than the decent measure of care that society is prepared to tolerate as adequate. I do not imply that one part of his single duty to his child rests on the general sentiment of society, and another part on his own thoughts and feelings. For him, the whole of the duty is one of individual morality and depends on his own thought. The point is that if an agent is not himself conscious of the factors giving rise to an obligation, and so does not have an obligation of individual morality, he may nevertheless be under an obligation in certain circumstances, and if so his obligation depends on the thought of society.

I come next to the second question, whether 'subjective duty' is to be made 'doubly subjective' or 'putative'. Here it is presupposed that obligation depends on the agent's thought. I have agreed that many obligations are so subjective. The question now is, whether the agent's duty is to do what would be in fact demanded by the situation assuming it to be what he thinks it is, or whether his duty is to do what he *judges* to be demanded by what he takes to be the situation. Here again, I think that, in practice at least, the first alternative should be re-phrased as 'what most people (or their appointed authority) would judge to be demanded'.

Now this second problem of 'putative duty' or 'the second dose of subjectivity'[1] arises, it seems to me, only where there is a conflict of obligations. Here, too, there is no cut-and-dried answer prescribing one of the alternatives for all cases. When we speak of the duty to follow one's own conscience, this is usually in difficult dilemmas of a conflict of obligations, where nobody finds it easy to decide which shall be deemed paramount. There is no firm view that is generally accepted, and we commonly think that the agent must decide for himself. Even in cases where it is evident that most people would judge differently from the agent, we recognize the fallibility of human judgement and often think it best that the agent should exercise his own initiative as a moral agent. But we are not always content to leave the judgement to the agent's conscience. For if one or more of the conflicting obligations concerned is a generally accepted obligation of social morality, then one or more 'objective' claims is involved, and the persons affected by the agent's action will not necessarily be content that he should be the arbiter of their claims. That an agent should exercise the initiative of moral judgement in determining his duty is very desirable. But that his judgement should determine the absence of a right in others may not be so desirable. To determine which obligation is the duty is to determine which claim is the right. If I told a creditor that his

[1]These descriptions are used by Dr. Carritt (*Ethical and Political Thinking*, ch. ii) and Sir David Ross (*Foundations of Ethics*, ch. vii) respectively.

moral claim to have his bill paid was overborne because, in my opinion, my child's claim to a new coat was stronger, he would not agree that my judgement determined the status of his claim. Or suppose a body of employees were told that their admittedly justifiable claim for an increase of pay was overborne, in their employers' opinion, by the claims of the firm's shareholders to greater profits; the employees would hardly agree that this opinion must be decisive. To be serious, I think most plain men would regard as monstrous the view, implied by the putative theory, that Hitler did his duty in sending people to gas chambers if (as seems quite likely) he genuinely believed that his paramount obligation was to aggrandize the German nation at any cost. Where the action will seriously affect the generally recognized claims of others, some of whom are unable to share or accept the agent's judgement on the issue, we prefer to trust the judgement of some impartial authority set up to give a decision.

In an organized society, claims of this kind are explicitly recognized in positive law or quasi-legal ordinances, so that authority to decide conflicts may be assigned to the judicature or some analogous body. Their decision determines, I should say, not only the legal but also the moral duty and right as between conflicting obligations and claims. But the decisions will be found acceptable as determinations of moral duty, only if the person or body of persons having authority to decide is generally thought to be impartial, approximating to the objectivity of general, as opposed to individual, moral judgement. If the courts of a national state merely reflect the arbitrary judgements of a tyrant, they are not accepted as authoritative or objective, though of course their *legal* authority within the existing system of law in that state may be perfectly valid. In the absence of a generally accepted authority, I think the determinant of 'objective' moral duty is the consensus of public opinion. The proposal that an explicit Convention of Human Rights be adopted, and that alleged breaches of human rights be submitted to the Court of International Justice, has arisen because there was no body empowered to express authoritatively the general judgement of the community of mankind concerning some of the acts of the Nazis that were permitted by the laws of the Nazi state. That general judgement does not only represent what would have been the Nazis' legal duty under international law if an international court had been empowered to express it and had in fact expressed it; it also determines what *was* the Nazis' moral duty, even though the Nazis themselves may have judged otherwise.

In our logic of moral concepts, a 'duty' was defined as either (1) an obligation in circumstances where there are no conflicting obligations, or (2) that obligation which is *judged,* amid a conflict of obligations, to be paramount or the strongest. In describing the second alternative, I did not specify *whose* judgement is in question, for usually it is the judgement of the agent but sometimes the judgement of what is taken to be an impartial authority. Again, in defining moral goodness in terms of duty, I said that a morally good man is one who acts *as he ought* and from the thought that he ought. I did not say 'acts as he *thinks* he ought', for while a man's duty is usually determined by his own judgement, sometimes it is not; and while the conscientious motive is always a necessary condition of moral goodness, it is not a sufficient condition. A conscience that is blind to 'the claims of our fellow-creatures' cannot give rise to moral goodness.[1] A moral agent must exercise 'autonomy', the initiative of judging for himself, but he is also subject to the 'legislation' of the 'realm of ends', and the content of moral judgement or 'legislation' is to treat others as ends-in-themselves. Like the freedom of 'enterprise', initiative in moral judgement lies with the individual under the condition that the commonly accepted claims of all members of a community are safeguarded. Where these may be breached by a decision, the determination of duty and right is not left to the individual agent.

[1]Cf. Hans Nystedt, 'The Problem of Duty and Knowledge', *Philosophy,* October, 1951, p. 346.

§7. *Conflicts of obligation*

Does our unifying principle provide us with a criterion for judging between conflicting obligations? I do not think it does. Since every obligation is a determinate form of the principle of treating persons as ends, a conflict of obligations means that we must fail to satisfy the principle in one respect in order to satisfy it in another. The principle is involved in each of the alternative acts and cannot be the guide for decision between them. The absence of a criterion for decision between conflicting obligations is a weakness of deontological theory, whether presented in the pluralistic form or in the unified Kantian form. The weakness is not an objection to deontological theory as a picture of ordinary moral judgement, for it simply reflects a practical difficulty found in ordinary life. Apart from disagreement on facts and on means to agreed ends, the main differences of opinion in moral and political judgement concern the comparative 'weight' attached to conflicting claims, and there seems to be no discernible criterion for decision. One person or group will attach greater importance to some element of justice, another to social utility, and so on. We cannot expect philosophy to resolve such disputes. But since philosophy aims at systematizing its data, it should try to indicate at least a theoretical solution of the difficulty.

It may be thought that utilitarianism has the advantage over deontological theory here. One of Sidgwick's reasons for abandoning the 'intuitional method' (as he called deontology) in favour of the utilitarian, was that the former gave us no criterion for choosing between conflicting 'intuitions' (i.e. common principles of obligation) while utilitarianism did. Where there is no conflict between common rules, he was content that we should follow the common rules; but where they fail to give us a standard for our judgement, he advised us to use the criterion of utility. I agree with Sidgwick that we need to go beyond the common principles of obligation in our moral theory, in order to make them coherent, but I think he was mistaken in supposing that utilitarianism provides a common foundation for all these principles and that it can supply a standard for decision between them when they conflict.

We have seen that the principle of utility will not do as a basis for justice. There, the Kantian principle of ends-in-themselves stands out in conflict with utility. To some extent this is recognized in utilitarian theory itself, and the impression that utilitarianism gives us a single principle as foundation and standard of moral judgement is illusory. Although utilitarians resolve some elements of justice into utility, they cannot treat the whole of the concept of justice in this way, and they accordingly leave one or more principles of equity or equality separate from the principle of maximizing the amount of happiness. Sidgwick, whose theory is far the most cogent version of utilitarianism, had several principles of 'equity' among his fundamental 'intuitions' that had to be accepted as self-evident.[1] Suppose we have the choice of two alternative courses of action; one will produce great happiness for one man or one small group of men, while the other will produce a slightly smaller total amount of happiness but distributed among several men or among a large group of men. Which of the two ought we to prefer? Are we to give preference to the principle of producing as much happiness as possible, or to the principle of spreading happiness as widely as possible? Utilitarianism gives us no supreme principle for deciding between these two. The hypothetical dilemma is not purely imaginary and unrealistic. A man may have the choice of spending his life in such a way as to give himself, or his family, great happiness, or of spending it so as to improve a little the lot of many unfortunates. I suppose Albert Schweitzer's choice looked something like this when he decided to leave Europe for Africa. Again, a government, in its fiscal policy, often has the choice of stimulating greater production of future wealth by means of incentives that will involve some inequity, or of bringing about less unequal shares of existing wealth at the expense of sacrificing some part of a future maximum of pro-

[1] *The Methods of Ethics* (7th edition), pp. 379 ff.

duction. How in such a conflict are we to decide which course of action is most strongly obligatory or 'best'? We cannot decide by the suggested utilitarian criterion of the maximum *amount* of total happiness to be produced, for *ex hypothesi* the first alternative in each of our examples seems likely to lead to that. The fact that we think the second possibility a real alternative shows that maximum happiness is not the sole consideration to be taken into account.

It may be said that ideal utilitarianism is not faced with the dilemma, for it prescribes the act that will produce most *good*. Now if we look at the two theories of ideal utilitarianism that were produced at the beginning of this century, the theories of Moore and Rashdall, we shall find that the problem of weighing equity against good results is not resolved. Moore simply neglected the problem. Rashdall[1] was very conscious of it in his valuable discussion of justice; 'it is a matter of life and death to our position', he said, to find a common denominator for justice and benevolence. His solution was to suggest that justice is itself good. But since he held, with most philosophers who have spoken of intrinsic goods, that goodness must be an attribute of states of mind and could not characterize the mere distribution enjoined by justice, he suggested that the goodness of justice lies in the disposition and will to distribute justly. Plainly this will not do as the foundation of the moral claims of justice. It implies that governments, and persons in authority generally, are to have regard to an equal distribution of good to the members of the community involved, because this realizes a good *in the governors,* namely their disposition to distribute justly. But obviously the distribution is to be justified by what it does to the recipients, not by what it produces in the distributors. It seems to me that if ideal utilitarianism is to avoid being *less* acceptable than hedonistic utilitarianism, it must retain the principle of equity as a separate one from that of producing a maximum of good, and in that case the dilemma of finding a common denominator would remain.

[1] *The Theory of Good and Evil,* Vol. I, pp. 266-7.

Oddly enough, the deontologist Ross[1] espouses the suggestion rejected by the agathist Rashdall, that a just distribution is itself intrinsically good. This, as Ross would agree, involves abandoning agathistic *utilitarianism,* and so indeed does Rashdall's suggestion, for both require us to take account of a goodness that does not lie in the *consequences* of the act. For Ross, the goodness of justice lies in a character of the act; for Rashdall, it lies in the goodness of the motive. Although Ross regards the rightness of justice as due to a non-instrumental goodness, he does not rest the rightness of all obligations on goodness. H. W. B. Joseph,[2] however, proposed a non-utilitarian theory of agathism which says that the rightness of all right actions is a form of goodness, but a different form in different kinds of right action; sometimes it is the character of causing good results, sometimes of having a good motive, and sometimes of being an element in a good pattern of life. This theory, like Rashdall's, gives a resolution of our problem in words, but only in words. We are offered the criterion of seeking the maximum amount of good, and are to compare the amounts of goodness in the alternative actions before us. But since their 'goodness' is of different forms, it is difficult to see what we are to compare as being homogeneous. In words there is homogeneity, since the different things to be compared are each called forms of 'good', but they are still different kinds of things. The deontologist likewise has verbal homogeneity, when he speaks of comparing the stringencies of different obligations. And in practice it makes not the slightest difference whether we say we must ask if the 'good' of keeping our promise or of equal distribution is greater than the good of happiness produced, or whether we say we must ask which of the obligations is stronger.

But, some agathists will say, there is a difference for theory. For good is a quality, and qualities admit of different degrees. Obligation, however, is a relation, and how can that have degrees? Joseph would not have put this objection, for he did not regard good as a quality, but it might be put by an agathist

[1] *The Right and the Good,* pp. 27, 138.
[2] *Some Problems in Ethics,* chaps. vii-viii.

who accepts Moore's view of good. As a positive argument for an agathistic theory it has very little force, for no-one, I should imagine, would say that promise-keeping has an intrinsic *quality* of goodness, the amount of which can be compared with the amount of good produced by a felicific act; and few people would say that a particular kind of distribution of goods has such an intrinsic quality. But although the argument does not give positive assistance to a wholly agathistic theory, can the deontologist meet the negative contention that the relation of obligation does not admit of degrees?

We say that obligations differ in strength or stringency. If the idea of moral obligation is one of being 'tied' to other persons, the bond can be closer or less close, tight or loose. These words are, of course, metaphors, but if our suggestion of how the metaphorical idea of a moral bond arises is acceptable, it enables us to explain why the concept includes the notion of degrees. The affective-conative side of sympathetic imagination can be more or less strong, and therefore it is natural that a concept arising from the experience of sympathetic imagination should include the idea of degree. It is perfectly possible for a 'relation' which is a state of mind directed to an object, to have degrees. Philosophers often call love and hate, for instance, 'relations' in this sense. Strictly speaking, the degrees attach to the experience as an affective-conative one, while the relation of being directed towards, or intended upon, an object belongs to the experience as a cognitive one. (Perhaps a conation that did not include cognition could also be directed to an object, but then it would not be an *experience*.) This does not imply, however, that the affection, conation, and cognition, are three separate experiences; they are all part of the one experience. At any rate, experiences like love, hate, and likewise sympathy, include all three, and therefore they can be both relational (or intentional) and characterized by degree.

This has not given us a criterion for determining the strength of obligations. It has simply disposed of the objection that agathistic terminology is more satisfactory than deontological because a quality may have degrees and a relation cannot. But perhaps it also enables us to suggest a theoretical criterion—not that this is likely to be of any assistance in practice. The suggestion is analogous to Adam Smith's doctrine of the 'impartial spectator', but, as elsewhere, my account uses as its basis the sympathetic imagination of the moral agent and not that of a spectator of action. The strongest obligation is that which we think an ideal moral agent would actually feel most strongly. What is meant here by an 'ideal' moral agent? One whose sympathetic imagination embraced all the interests that the alternative acts would affect directly or indirectly. This looks like a utilitarian criterion after all. But I am not saying that the ideal agent's judgement would depend on the total amount of satisfaction that each act would cause. It would depend on the relative strength of his sympathies, and these would be affected by factors additional to the degree and extent of the interests involved. (Degree and extent of the interests involved form the criterion for *fitting* action). For instance, one additional factor is that sympathy for close associates is naturally stronger than sympathy for strangers. Another factor, counteracting the stress on familiars to the relative neglect of strangers, is that an ideal agent would feel strongly those claims which are generally recognized as due, in justice, to everyone within a community (and sometimes this is a limited community, sometimes the community of mankind) regardless of individual circumstances.

The conception of such an ideal agent is of course hopelessly vague, and it would be absurd to suggest that an individual, let alone a publicly appointed authority, in deciding between conflicting claims, should try to imagine how this ideal agent would feel. In practice, judges follow their idea of the paths laid down (in the spirit as well as in the letter of the law) by their predecessors, and thereby themselves contribute to the guidance available to their successors. Individuals follow their 'lights', which may occasionally be guided in part by the thought of how some admired figure of the past or present would have acted, but which usually owe much, in a less conscious way, to tradition and to the sympathies aroused by their own past experience and observation. I do not mean that a genetic explanation, in terms of unconscious influences, gives the whole of the story. If a man is actively trying to resolve a moral dilemma, he is not just passively affected by past influences. The process is in part passive and in part active. The active element in the judgement is, like the adoption of a general policy of action, a commitment for the future and a recommendation for others. I do not think it is a wholly irrational leap in the dark. It is rather an experiment guided by the thought that one of the alternative acts will, when its results are seen, satisfy the sympathies of the agent himself and of the community of moral agents more than the other alternative would have done. When we see the results, we may feel confirmed in our judgement, or we may feel that the other alternative would have satisfied more the sympathies of the 'ideal agent', i.e. of one who could form an accurate idea of the results beforehand. In the latter event, we, and others who are able to profit by our 'experiment', will try the alternative 'experiment' when faced with an apparently similar dilemma in the future.

Both with judges and with individual moral agents, the resolution of a moral dilemma does not emanate solely from the person now judging, nor is its effect limited to his present decision on the situation now confronting him. It owes something to past experience, of himself and of others, and his own contribution will have its effect on future judgements, both of himself and of others. Just as the status of claimants as ends-in-themselves rests partly on their nature as individuals and partly on their membership of a community of moral persons, so the judgement of the moral agent, both in its origin and in its contribution, is related both to his individual sympathies and commitments, and to the tradition of the community of moral agents within which he makes his moral assessments. Individual 'experiment' is not tolerated where it seriously invades rights the supremacy of which is considered, by the general community of moral persons, to be beyond doubt. But where there is doubt, a variety of 'experiment' is to be encouraged. The value of individual initiative in judgement lies not only in enhancing the sense of responsibility for the results of our act, but also in providing evidence for future judgements. *Solvitur ambulando.*

VIII

EPISTEMOLOGY AND ETHICS

§1. *Epistemology and metaphysics*

The relations within a 'language' or system of concepts and propositions are the subject-matter of logic or 'syntactics'. The relation of 'language' or thought to fact is the subject-matter of epistemology or 'semantics'. Part of the discussion of the previous chapter is epistemological. But a theory of knowledge or epistemology presupposes a theory of fact or ontology. At the one extreme is the view that whatever is the object of intentional meaning is an entity. The advocate of this view is prepared to give subsistent status to universals and propositions of all kinds, including the propositions of imagination and perhaps even self-contradictory propositions. For him there is no epistemological problem. An object of thought is what it is and not another thing. If we may think of a centaur, there are subsistent centaurs. If we may think that an act is right, there is a subsistent quality of rightness. At the other extreme is the view of the phenomenalistic solipsist that the only entities are his own fragmentary data of experience. For him the epistemological problem is immense, since he must relate all concepts and propositions to his limited and transient experience.[1]

Rationalism and empiricism are regarded primarily as theories of knowledge, but they involve theories about the nature of reality—or at least methodological principles of what shall be regarded as fact for the purposes of epistemology. The rationalist holds that reality is that which is disclosed in faultless thought, the empiricist that it is the data of experience, by which he usually means sensation and feeling. A

[1]Cf. E. Gellner, 'Analysis and Ontology', *The Philosophical Quarterly*, October, 1951, p. 411.

rationalist theory of knowledge is an account of the criteria distinguishing knowledge or faultless thought, in which fact is directly revealed, from opinion or fallible thought, which has an indirect relation to fact; the relation of opinion to knowledge will show the relation of the objects of opinion (namely propositions) to the objects of knowledge (namely facts). An empiricist theory of knowledge is an account of the relation of propositions and concepts (Hume would say 'ideas', his present-day successors would say 'language') to experience. My account of 'the nature of' moral obligation and fittingness has been of the latter kind, except that I do not confine experience to sensation and feeling. But my purpose was not to give a detailed account of the *relation* between moral concepts and experience, simply presupposing the empiricist ontology. It was rather to seek the 'facts', to which the concepts of morals are related. I was led to locate these 'facts' in human experience through trying to understand just what is meant by Kant's principle of treating persons as ends-in-themselves. I have therefore called my discussion metaphysical rather than epistemological.

Epistemological discussion has occupied a prominent place in recent ethical theory, as it did among the British moralists of the eighteenth century. Such discussion has a direct bearing on properly ethical issues only to the extent that it has metaphysical implications. I shall try to show in this chapter that epistemological discussion of moral judgements, if divorced from the metaphysical implications of general epistemological theories, settles none of the main issues that have been thought to be involved in the debate about reason and feeling in moral judgement.

Rationalists have argued that moral judgement can express strict knowledge, and have often compared it with the knowledge of mathematical truths. Their purpose in undertaking to show this has been to prove that ethical concepts stand directly for characteristics of reality. Knowledge, they have argued, is of fact, and therefore if moral judgements can be expressions of knowledge, what they assert when they do express knowledge is objective fact. If this argument were sound, our inquiry into the 'facts' of ethics, into the nature of obligation and fittingness, could be quickly completed. If I, at least sometimes, have knowledge when I judge that I am under an obligation, then what I judge is a fact. And if, as we have argued in Part I, the concept of obligation is not a complex of other notions but is to be taken as an ultimate ethical notion, then it simply stands for a peculiar characteristic of reality. Moral obligation just is a unique kind of thing, and there is nothing more to be said about it than what is found in the intentional meaning of a moral judgement expressing knowledge.

This is the position of ethical intuitionism, which relies on a rationalist-realist theory of knowledge in the tradition of Aristotle, Descartes, and, coming nearer home, Cook Wilson. Professor Prichard's well known article 'Does Moral Philosophy rest on a Mistake?'[1] uses Cook Wilson's theory of knowledge as the starting-point for critical discussion of moral philosophy. In that article, Prichard holds that the theory of knowledge arose from asking the question, how can we prove that we know, how can we justify knowledge, i.e., justify it by something else? The question is pointless, for it is by knowledge that we prove other things. Knowledge is the criterion of proof and so cannot be itself subject to proof. Moral philosophy, Prichard argues, arose with a similar question, how can we prove that we ought to do our duties, or, how can we justify duty, i.e., justify it by something else, such as our interest? This question, too, is pointless. For it presupposes that we know certain actions to be our duty, what we ought to do, and yet asks for a proof that we ought to do them, a proof based on something other than the knowledge that we ought to do them. Prichard says the error is similar to that involved in the theory of knowledge. But in view of the reason he gives for the pointlessness of the question of traditional moral philosophy, namely that it asks for a proof of what it at the same time takes to be knowledge and so incapable of proof, he

[1] *Mind*, 1912; reprinted in *Moral Obligation*.

would have done better to say that the mistake of traditional moral philosophy was a specific instance or application of the general mistake of the theory of knowledge.

Prichard's argument against traditional moral philosophy includes the premiss that the formulation of the traditional question assumes that we *know* what actions we ought to do while yet asking for a proof that we ought to do these actions. Now whether or not traditional moral philosophy did make that assumption, it is an assumption that can be questioned. Disagreement in moral judgement suggests that we do not know for certain what are the actions we ought to do. But the epistemological discussions of moral philosophers, both in the eighteenth and in the twentieth centuries, have owed less to practical difficulties of this kind than to the grinding of metaphysical axes. The intuitionist, who believes that reality is characterized by a necessity which is not read into facts by thought but is apprehended as already there, compares moral judgement with mathematical in order to show that in our moral judgements we apprehend reality with its necessary truths. The empiricist, who believes that reality consists of contingent events, and that the intuition of objective necessity (or 'synthetic *a priori* judgement') is a myth, argues that moral judgements are not the expression of knowledge but of feeling. Now the empiricist is prepared to agree that mathematical judgement expresses 'knowledge' of necessity, but he holds that it is analytic, that the necessity is contributed by the procedures adopted in mathematical thinking, and not by objective fact; a system of mathematical propositions has the same necessity whether it applies to the world of fact or not. But it has not occurred to him to argue that the same might be true of moral judgement. This seems to be obviously synthetic, and so he denies that it expresses knowledge. Otherwise, he thinks, he would be compelled to admit the bogy of the synthetic *a priori*. So far as ethical judgements are concerned, he is implicitly *accepting* the rationalist doctrine that judgements expressing strict knowledge state facts.

Although the ethical intuitionist's premiss that moral

judgements express knowledge can be challenged, the crucial point of his argument lies in his *metaphysical* doctrine that judgements expressing 'strict knowledge' (e.g. mathematical judgements) state facts, disclose the nature of things. If we were to deny this doctrine, as the empiricist does when talking about mathematics, then a sound argument to the effect that moral judgements express knowledge (or are 'judgements of reason') would not carry us to the 'facts' of morality.

When we say, in ordinary language, that we know, we undoubtedly imply that we cannot be mistaken, that what we have before our mind is a fact and not a hypothesis. A rationalist would claim that it is a self-evident truth that knowledge is of fact; the proposition is for him one of those synthetic *a priori* judgements whose existence is in dispute. If a latter-day empiricist were to accept explicitly the proposition that knowledge is of fact, he would certainly not appeal to any metaphysical insight but would be likely to appeal to the authority of ordinary language. Now if the appeal to the usage of ordinary language is simply an empirical appeal, the conclusion to be reached is merely one of the *logical* relationship between words or concepts in a system of language. The use of the verb 'know' before a substantival clause implies that the object of the verb may be described by the noun 'fact'.

The rationalist takes logical relationships to reflect ontological relationships, but he does not do so on the naïve ground that the plain man's use of language is always correct, or that the plain man's thought, expressed in his use of language, is always true. The rationalist claims that reflection on the metaphysical beliefs of the plain man, which are represented in the usages of ordinary language, can show that some of those beliefs are justified while others are not. He may conclude, for example, that plain men are mistaken in thinking that perception gives knowledge, and consequently he would hold that they *misuse* the word 'know' when they make a statement like 'I know the ball is in that shrub; I saw it land there'. For the rationalist, some of the things which the plain man says he knows may indeed be known; mathematical truths, for instance. But other things which the plain man says he knows, are not known but only believed.

If an empiricist agrees that knowledge is of fact, is he stating a logical or a metaphysical relationship? If he merely means that the usages of ordinary language permit us to describe as 'a fact' the proposition expressed by a substantival clause when that clause is the object of the verb 'know', what he is saying is true but trivial. But then, if he is simply concerned with the logic of ordinary language, why should he be at such pains to deny that moral judgements express knowledge since they are 'really' expressions of feelings, or 'attitudes', or advice, or anything on earth so long as it is not knowledge of fact? One cannot doubt that plain men often *say* 'I know that this is the right thing to do'. The conclusion seems irresistible that a philosopher who agrees that knowledge must be of fact, and adds that ethical judgements do not express knowledge because that would imply the existence of peculiar non-natural entities, is accepting the *metaphysical* theory reflected in the logical relationships between the ordinary usage of the words 'know' and 'fact'. And since, for the empiricist, fact or reality is experience, the statement that knowledge is of fact means that the object of knowledge is experience. In his view, however, the relation of 'fact' to knowledge is usually not that of being the *direct* object of knowledge, as it is for the rationalist. A mathematical truth is not itself a piece of experience, nor is a material thing. Our knowledge of mathematical truths and material things stands in a complicated, indirect relation to the 'facts' that make it knowledge. Then why should the empiricist shy at saying that moral judgements express knowledge? There, too, the experience which is the 'real fact' need not be the direct object of the judgment as the rationalist would wish to say it is. The empiricist accepts the statement of the plain man that he knows twice two make four, but does not regard this as requiring him to accept the rationalist thesis that the mathematical truth is a subsistent entity. He can therefore accept the plain man's statement that he knows it is right to keep promises without accepting the view that the moral principle is a subsistent entity.

If the empiricist objects to having metaphysical doctrines ascribed to him, we may alternatively put his position thus. His concern in philosophy is to examine the relation of language or thought to experience. If he does not want to talk about what is real and what is not, he should treat 'fact' as a word and no more, a word which, in the commonly used system of language, has a logical relationship to other words like 'know' and 'true'. The proposition 'knowledge is of fact' should be, for him, a proposition of logic and not of epistemology. His epistemological propositions about knowledge are concerned with the relation of the *word* 'knowledge' to *experience* (not to the *word* 'experience' or the word 'fact' or any other word or set of words). Then if the relation of the word 'knowledge' to experience is queer and complicated with perceptual 'knowledge', and is queer and complicated in a different way with mathematical 'knowledge', he should be prepared to allow the same of moral 'knowledge'. That is, he should see that a description of moral judgement as 'knowledge' does not necessarily wreck the methodological principles which he follows in his philosophy.

What the empiricist is concerned to deny, in his epistemological discussion of moral judgements, is the metaphysical doctrine that there are entities in the world which can be the direct objects of an experience called intuition, an experience superior to other forms of ordinary human experience in that its data are not contingent events but necessary and universal entities transcending time and space. The question whether moral judgement may properly be described as 'knowledge' does not settle this metaphysical issue. For the rationalist holds that the entities in dispute include mathematical truths, and the empiricist denies that mathematical truths are subsistent entities while agreeing that mathematical judgement may properly be called knowledge. When the rationalist argues that moral judgements may express knowledge, he means the sort of knowledge expressed by mathematical judgements. He often describes it as 'strict knowledge' in order to distinguish it from judgements (e.g., assured perceptual judgements) which the plain man would describe as knowledge but which the rationalist would call belief or opinion; here the usage of the plain man, according to rationalist doctrine, is loose and inaccurate. But if the question whether mathematical truths are subsistent entities is not settled by determining whether mathematical judgements express 'strict' or incorrigible knowledge, then a comparison between moral and mathematical judgement will not settle the question whether rightness and goodness are subsistent entities. If we assume a rationalist theory of the relation of knowledge to reality, the comparison permits an inference that the objects of moral judgement must be real entities. But if we do not assume the rationalist theory of knowledge, we simply have, both in mathematical and in moral judgement, a certain kind of objects of cognition. I have not yet considered whether the analogy between mathematical and moral judgement is justified. But if it is, it will not settle any metaphysical issue.

§2. *Epistemology and psychology*

The interest of contemporary empiricists in moral philosophy is almost wholly confined to epistemological discussion of moral judgements. Some of them call their inquiry the 'logic' of ethical words and pose its problem in some such form as this: 'How do ethical words function or "behave"? In what sort of circumstances do we use the words "right", "good", etc?' I suppose that this kind of inquiry is called 'logic' because it is concerned with the use or function of language. It is an examination of language in relation to the circumstances of its use, as opposed to an examination of the intentional meaning before the mind of the user. I am reserving the name 'logic' for the study of the interrelations between concepts and propositions in their intentional meaning. An examination of 'meaning' by reference to the circumstances of the use of words is concerned with the relation of language to the facts of experience, and this is epistemology.

In considering the relation of language to experience, what we allow to be experience is a matter of dispute. A positivistic empiricist may hold that experience is limited to sensation and feeling, and that cognitive and conative words express combinations of sensations and feelings in the form of 'dispositions'; that is to say, cognitive and conative words are shorthand for comprehensive statements of what sort of experiences (i.e. sensations and feelings) would be had by the person said to 'know' or 'desire', and by observers of his behaviour, in a cluster of possible types of situation vaguely adumbrated in the expression used. But we may take a wider view of experience than that. We may hold that there are actual cognitive and conative experiences as well as sensations and affections. If so, I think we must allow that cognition and conation are a different kind of experience from the kind allowed by positivists. One way of putting the difference is to say that sensation and affection are passive, while cognition and conation are active. Another way of putting the difference is to say that sensations and affections may be made objects of observation, the kind of observation that psychologists call introspection; cognitions and conations cannot be made objects of introspection, for they are activities that we 'live through' and not data 'impressed' upon us. (They can perhaps be later 'retrospected' as 'impressions' of memory, but what is then the object of our inspection is an effect of the activity and not the activity itself.) On this view, Hume was right to confine 'impressions' to the data of sense and feeling, but wrong to think that all 'ideas' or concepts must arise from such impressions alone. At any rate, if we allow that cognitive and conative experiences occur, we can include them in our epistemological discussions, i.e. in our discussions of the relation of language or concepts to experience. But cognitive and conative activities, if they exist, are intentional; cognitive activities have objects or contents of meaning, and conative activities have objectives or ends. It follows that there can be an examination of intentional meaning, of language from 'the inside', as well as an examination of linguistic 'behaviour', i.e. an examination of language from 'the outside' in relation to its environment of feeling and sensation in the person using the language and in others who observe his use of language. In my view, logic is concerned with relationships in intentional meaning; epistemology is concerned with the relation of intentional meaning to experience.

If we allow that there are cognitive and conative activities, we may say that moral judgement can include such experiences. But if we take the narrower view of experience, we must say that moral judgement is, in the end, a function of feeling or sensation and nothing more. A book on moral philosophy is not called upon to determine issues of general epistemology. Must we, however, say that one's view of the epistemology of morals will depend on one's general epistemological theory and that is that? Must we say that empiricists of the narrow school and their opponents cannot possibly agree on the epistemology of morals, and that there is no point in either side trying to convince the other in the specific field of ethics? That they must do their convincing, if it can be done at all, in general epistemology, and then agreement in ethics will follow as a matter of course but cannot come without agreement in the general field?

Recent discussion of ethics might suggest this conclusion. There is no doubt that intuitionists and emotivists in ethics disagree basically in their general epistemological views. Professor Prichard and his followers accepted ethical intuitionism along with intuitionism in the theory of knowledge. Professor Ayer was obliged, in *Language, Truth and Logic,* to give an emotive account of ethics because he had adopted a narrow empiricist doctrine in general epistemology and because acceptance of the view that there is a kind of knowledge 'which relates to question of value' would present 'an insuperable objection' to his 'radical empiricist thesis'.[1]

The metaphysical dispute in ethics about non-natural

[1] 2nd edition, p. 102.

entities is certainly tied up with the metaphysical implications of rationalist and empiricist epistemologies. But I do not think that difference of opinion in general epistemology need preclude agreement on the question whether moral judgement is simply a matter of feeling or is also rational. The ethical rationalist has tried to show that moral judgement is like mathematical judgement and is therefore rational or a species of knowledge. I think it is quite easy to show that some moral judgements are like mathematical judgements in the respect relevant for applying the descriptions 'rational' and 'knowledge'. But, if my argument for the analogy is satisfactory, I do not see why an empiricist should not accept it while yet retaining his general theory of knowledge. For he can still go on to say that the description of such judgement as a form of 'knowing', while legitimate enough, does not imply that there is an *experience* called knowing. He does, after all, admit that 'know' is a word legitimately applied in other circumstances. He holds, however, that when it is so applied, it is a way either of describing the assertion of an analytic proposition or of referring to a disposition to have, or to present to others by one's behaviour, sensitive or affective experiences in certain circumstances. A rationalist, of course, will not accept this account of 'knowing'. But *that* is a dispute for general epistemology, and ethics can leave it to be debated there. The question at issue in ethics is whether any moral judgements are correctly described as 'knowing', i.e. whether they are like mathematical judgements in those respects which are the rationalist's criterion for distinguishing mathematical judgement, as 'knowing', from e.g. perceptual judgement or a judgement of taste. An affirmative answer to this question will not settle the question whether knowing is a cognitive *experience;* that is a matter for general epistemology. Nor will it settle the question whether the objects of 'strict knowing' are real entities; that is a matter for metaphysics.

It may be argued that once we admit, with the rationalists, the existence of cognitive acts, the metaphysical doctrine that knowledge is of reality can be proved from an examination of the act of knowing. Professor Prichard held that when we know, we know that we know. His appeal was not to the logical implications of ordinary usage but to philosophical reflection, which could tell us when the plain man's use of 'know' was right and when it was wrong. We can find out whether the word 'know' is appropriate by putting ourselves in a position where it would ordinarily be said that we know something, and then considering whether we really know. If we do really know, we shall know that we know, and shall know that we know reality.

The doctrine looks like an appeal to introspection, but this presumption is illusory, for cognitive acts cannot become objects of introspection. I should agree that we have an awareness of cognitive acts, but it is not the awareness of an object. We 'live through' or 'enjoy' the performance of a cognitive act, but we cannot hold it before us as an object and scrutinize characteristics of the act that differentiate it from another kind of cognitive act. The distinction between knowing and believing is not made from a comparison of the *acts* of knowing and believing. As Plato realized,[1] we can distinguish between different kinds of cognition only by reference to *their* objects and their effects. We are aware of having a cognitive experience, but that awareness will not itself tell us whether the experience is knowing or believing, i.e., whether it is incorrigible or corrigible. So far as the mere *Erlebnis* is concerned, there is no difference between knowing and believing; and they may both be accompanied by the strongest possible degree of the feeling of conviction. The 'analysis' of different types of cognition is a classification of them under different names by reference to differences in their objects and effects. What the rationalist calls 'strict knowledge' is a cognition the object of which is a *necessary* proposition. He therefore says that mathematical judgement is 'strict knowing', and he assumes that necessity, in a proposition which is not psychologically analytic, is contributed by reality. If the proposition that forms the object of a cognitive act is not a necessary pro-

[1] *Republic*, 477d.

position, he says that the cognition is not knowledge but belief or opinion. The other criterion, relating to the effects of a cognition, is pragmatic. If a perceptual judgement that the cricket ball landed in the mulberry bush enables me to pursue successfully my purpose of retrieving the ball, the rationalist will call the judgement true belief and the plain man will often call it knowledge. If the judgement lets me down in pursuing my purpose, both will call it false belief. Since the rationalist assumes that the necessity of 'strict knowledge' is contributed by reality, he will usually assume that knowledge, like true belief, will enable us to be successful in dealing with things. But if, for example, an astronomer finds that the use of Euclidean geometry, in calculating spatial relations between heavenly bodies at great distances from each other, leads to results that conflict with his observations, the rationalist is inclined to say, not that Euclidean geometry does not apply to reality after all, but that some of the observations, or the interpretation of them, must be mistaken. He prefers the criterion of necessity to the pragmatic criterion. But in either event the criterion for distinguishing knowledge from fallible belief does not lie in the nature of the cognitive act.

When we ask whether moral judgement is a function of reason or feeling, the inquiry looks like a psychological one. It would seem that the simplest way to find out is to look within and see. Now if we admit that there are cognitive experiences, the psychological test will show whether there is such an experience but it will not show whether the experience is one of knowing. The rationalist case in ethics looks weak when presented as if it were an appeal to introspection of an 'intuition' or act of knowing. In pointing to the deficiencies of opposing views, rationalists have admittedly been on strong ground. But their positive argument has been given in vague terms which suggest that what they are doing is looking within and finding intuition. Their opponents say that they can find no such thing. The dispute is at a deadlock because the criteria for reaching a view are given the appearance of being psychological. But in fact the disputants rely on non-psychological arguments. They need no careful introspection to agree that there is an experience of feeling. The question is whether intuition occurs also. The emotivist does not really bother to look carefully within and see if he can find intuition. He does not bother, because he is convinced at the start that intuition is a myth. On the other side, the intuitionist does indeed use a psychological test for the existence of a cognition, but it needs no careful scrutiny to be conscious of that. The careful scrutiny is given to the question whether the cognition is knowledge or merely opinion, and is directed at the object of the cognitive act, not at the act itself. Professor Prichard often used to announce his findings of knowledge with some such phrase as, 'When we reflect, we see that . . .'. His careful 'reflection' was not introspection of his state of mind. He would have said, I think, that reflection showed him what was, and what was not, self-evident.

The impression that the intuitionist's criterion is psychological is partly due to the associations of the word 'intuition'. In addition to its popular and mystical uses, it has been employed by many philosophers to distinguish *immediate* judgement from discursive, and this has sometimes led them to extend the use of the word to immediate judgements which are fallible. Thomas Reid, for instance, used the word in this way. Dr. Ewing, who has been one of the staunchest advocates of ethical intuitionism in recent years, also uses 'intuition' in the extended sense to cover corrigible as well as incorrigible immediate judgements.[1] This is because Dr. Ewing, unlike most philosophers of the rationalist-realist tradition, does not make an absolute distinction between knowledge and belief.[2] But the philosophers of the rationalist tradition who have distinguished incorrigible knowledge from corrigible belief and have sometimes said that knowledge rests on 'intuition', have not used a psychological criterion. Their view has been that where there is rational intuition there is *necessary* truth. The

[1]Cf. *The Definition of Good*, pp. 26 ff; *Idealism*, p. 270, footnote; *Reason and Intuition*, pp. 12, 25.

[2]Cf. *Idealism*, p. 205.

warrant for the use of the label 'intuition' or 'strict knowledge', in the tradition that makes a distinction of kind between 'strict knowledge' and 'belief' or 'opinion', simply *is* the necessary truth of the object of cognition. At any rate, if we can agree that in some moral judgements the proposition asserted is necessarily true, then we can agree that the label used for mathematical judgements, whether it be 'knowledge', 'intuition', or anything else, is suitable for these moral judgements. For the purpose of the label will simply be to say that what such judgements assert is necessary as are the propositions of mathematics.

§3. *Moral judgement and reason*

An analogy between moral and mathematical judgement will be satisfactory only if the necessity of the moral propositions is similar to that of mathematical propositions. Empiricists hold that the necessity of mathematical propositions is analytic or 'tautological', and they must be able to say the same of moral propositions before they will allow that there is any proper analogy. This does not mean that our necessary moral propositions must be tautologies in the popular, psychological sense, in which 'Eggs are eggs' is a tautology and '$21 + 54 = 75$' is not. If a rationalist wants to say that the necessity of mathematical propositions is synthetic, he may say the same of the necessities of moral propositions. But if the sort of considerations which lead an empiricist to say that mathematical propositions are analytic can be held to apply to the moral propositions too, the empiricist may call them analytic if he chooses. I take it that the empiricist's argument for calling mathematical propositions analytic is that they follow from the definitions and postulates of the system in which they occur. When the rationalist calls them synthetic, he may have in mind the fact that the propositions themselves, and the inferences in which they figure as premisses or conclusions, are psychologically synthetic. Mathematical propositions are not tautologies in the sense in which 'Eggs are eggs' is a tautology, and few of them are analytic in the sense in which 'Grey horses are grey' is analytic. Similarly, few mathematical inferences rely solely on implications that are psychologically analytic like 'If p and q are true, then p is true'. It is probable, however, that the rationalist objects less to the extension of the labels 'tautologous' and 'analytic' beyond their psychological sense, than to the doctrine that the axioms of mathematics are merely postulates. In any event, if the rationalist means by 'synthetic *a priori* judgement' what is found in mathematics, then the empiricist may still be led to agree that certain moral judgements are what the rationalist would call synthetic *a priori* though he himself would call them analytic. What he is asked to agree to is that some moral judgements are like mathematical judgements in asserting propositions that are necessary and universal and that have relations of necessary connexion with other universal propositions.

The two parties will still differ, in general epistemology, over the label to be attached to mathematical and similar necessity, whether it is to be called 'analytic' or 'synthetic'. And they will still differ, in the metaphysic of mathematics and morals, on the question whether the axioms are only postulates, to which there can be alternatives with alternative systems of necessary propositions flowing from them. The empiricist need not agree that, because certain moral propositions are necessary, or follow necessarily from other propositions, they must reflect 'objective truth' or 'correspond to the nature of things' or (as he would perhaps prefer to say) are the only set of propositions applicable to the facts they are intended to order. For he may say, as he says of mathematics, that a system of propositions may be hypothetically necessary yet not applicable to the world of experience, or that alternative systems, each internally necessary, may be applicable to the same set of facts. Just as there may be alternative geometries, so there may be alternative moralities.

It is hard to maintain that all moral thinking is analogous to mathematical. For when obligations conflict, we are often in doubt and different individuals and groups differ in their judgements of duty. In an earlier book,[1] in which I accepted the metaphysical implications of rationalism, I suggested that decision between conflicting obligations is rather like the 'weighing' of evidence in empirical thinking; it is not the intuition or deduction of a necessity. The result of the process is accordingly belief or opinion and not knowledge. Mr. P. F. Strawson,[2] criticizing the intuitionist views of that book, has objected that, in order to pick out inductively a duty from conflicting obligations, I must have known, in other cases, what was my duty amid a conflict of obligations, and this means that I must then have picked it out non-inductively. I think that the theory of the present book escapes that particular objection. To pick out a duty from conflicting obligations is simply to pick out the obligation judged strongest. Provided that it is possible to make a non-inductive comparison on some occasions between the strength of felt obligations, it is possible to judge inductively on other occasions that one obligation is to be deemed stronger than another. We have seen, in Chapter VII, §7, that a decision between conflicting obligations cannot be deduced from a general principle, and I have suggested that it is derived inductively from the experience of feeling one sympathy to be stronger than a conflicting sympathy.

But I should still hold, as I maintained in the earlier book, that the judgement of a general principle of obligation asserts a necessary connexion—though I should not now imply the metaphysical doctrine that the proposition therefore reflects a feature of reality. When we think of general moral principles, e.g., 'One ought to relieve pain of which one is aware', 'One ought to keep promises', 'One can only have an obligation to do an action if it is within's one's power', they present themselves as asserting necessary implications. In fact, the existence or possibility of a *logic* of morals, i.e., a coherent system of concepts and universal propositions having implications with each other, shows that the use of these concepts and propositions involves 'reason'; this is a tautology. The implications are

[1] *The Moral Sense*, ch. vi.
[2] *Philosophy*, April, 1948, pp. 170-1.

not confined to the non-ethical terms in the sentences used. The ethical terms themselves have implications, as we have seen.

Our argument does not necessarily require the admission of synthetic implications in a sense objectionable to the empiricist. All the implications may be 'analytic' in the sense in which those of a mathematical system may be called analytic. The principle that one ought to keep a promise is clearly analytic in that obligation to perform is included in the meaning of 'promising' to perform; to promise is to 'bind oneself' to do an action. Likewise, 'ought' implies 'can' because the meaning of 'ought' includes the idea that the action proposed is within the power of the agent; we should not say he 'ought' if we did not think he could. In these examples, the necessary connexion follows from the definitions of the terms used. But what of principles like 'One ought to relieve pain of which one is aware'? This is not psychologically analytic. My suggestion is that the necessity of such principles is due to their being implied by the general 'axiom' of treating persons as ends. Whether we are to call them 'analytic' (in the empiricist's extended sense of that word) or 'synthetic *a priori*' depends on whether or not we regard the axiom as a postulate.

Our theory of moral obligation in the previous chapter has attempted to show that all these, psychologically synthetic, principles of moral obligation are determinate forms of the fundamental obligation to treat persons as ends, and that in this basic principle the obligation is to make the ends of others our own, i.e., to act as one would naturally act if one were the other person concerned. We said that the idea of moral obligation arises from an imaginative joining of personalities, an inter-personal relation of thinking of another's interests as if they were our own. Now to be conscious of one's own interests leads naturally to attempting to satisfy them. To be sympathetically aware of another's interests need not lead naturally to attempting to satisfy them; but to 'make them one's own ends' requires (by the *quasi-logical* imperative of making actions consistent with ends proposed) that we choose to satisfy them. That is to say, we 'ought' to satisfy them in the sense in which we 'ought' to take the appropriate steps to satisfy an end of our own where the action would not inevitably follow, e.g. because inhibited by a pressing impulse. Then if, from the adoption of an end and the calculation of means to that end, it 'follows' that we are (non-morally) required to choose the means, in the same sense the moral obligation to do a particular action leading to the satisfaction of the ends of others will follow from the adoption of the basic principle of obligation that we treat the ends of others as our own. If the implication in the former case may be called analytic, so may it in the latter. Whether the implication in either case *should* be called analytic is a question for general epistemology. The point for our purpose is that a similar implication exists in both types of instance.

It should be noted that I am not claiming that the ultimate principle of morals, the principle that we ought to treat other persons as ends in the way we naturally treat ourselves as ends, is a logically necessary principle. This principle is neither true by definition nor an implicate of a more ultimate principle. One could of course say that to be moral means to treat other persons as ends, and that therefore the proposition 'One is morally obliged to treat other persons as ends' is true by definition; but then we should still be left with the ultimate imperative 'Be moral'. My suggestion is that the ultimate principle is a postulate, a general policy of action, to which there could be alternatives. But if the policy is adopted, then specific manifestations of it, or means to implementing it, are implied as imperatives of action, just as the adoption of a universal premiss implies, as an imperative of thought, the acceptance of instances falling under it. (I use the word 'adopt' in the same sense for both types of example, namely, '*elect* to use' for the purposes of action or thought, as the case may be.) If we adopt Euclid's axioms, we are logically required to accept the theorems of his geometry. But just as there are alternative axioms, with alternative systems flowing from them, so there may be alternative policies of action to that of morality as we understand it.

It should also be noted that my comparison between the relation of a particular moral obligation to the ultimate principle of morals and the relation of a hypothetical imperative to an adopted end, does not mean that I am reducing the 'ought' of a particular moral obligation to the non-moral 'ought'. The moral 'ought' of the ultimate principle is carried over to the particular obligation. My view is that the original moral 'ought', as found in the comprehensive principle, cannot be analysed into a non-moral 'ought'; its function is to distinguish between prudential and moral policies. But the specific principles, and the particular obligations which exemplify them, can be 'derived', by use of the quasi-logical or non-moral 'ought', from the generic principle, in the way that the hypothetical imperative to use a means can be derived from the adoption of a (selfish or other) purpose and the understanding that the proposed action is a necessary means to fulfilling that purpose. Thus the 'ought' of a specific moral imperative includes both the moral 'ought', derived from the generic principle, and the quasi-logical or non-moral 'ought'. As including the quasi-logical 'ought', the specific imperative may be said to be 'implied' by the 'premisses'. That 'premiss' which consists of the generic principle of morals, however, is not a logically necessary proposition. Its place in the moral system is that of an ultimate postulate.

Even if our suggested unification of the various principles of obligation by means of Kant's principle of ends is unacceptable, the fact still remains that some of the principles commonly recognized have implicative relations with each other, implications flowing from their ethical terms as well as from their non-ethical terms. This in itself is sufficient to justify the view that moral judgement includes *a priori* thinking. To say that moral judgements are rational is simply to recognize the possibility of a logic of morals. It does not prove anything about the facts to which moral judgements refer, but merely points out that moral judgements employ universal propositions and concepts with logical relations between them. The examination of these relations has been the main concern of ethical rationalists in their debates about the right and the good, deontology and utilitarianism.

Empiricist theories of moral judgement deal with quite a different matter, the relation of ethical language or concepts to experience. They presuppose a particular theory of reality, and attempt to account for the rise of moral concepts from what they take to be real. Too often empiricists have confused what they are doing with an account of the logic of morals. It will not do to present a naturalistic theory as a theory of the *meaning* of ethical terms, to say that '*X* is right' *means* 'I approve of *X*' or 'Most people approve of *X*', or to present it (in the way that the expressive version of naturalism was at first presented) as a denial of meaning, as saying that '*X* is right' *means* nothing. To present a theory of the meaning of ethical terms is part of the logic of morals, and there the facts with which our theory must accord are what people making moral judgements have before their minds. A sensible naturalistic theory should be one like Hume's. He tries to build up, by reference to the natural feelings of sympathy and approval, to utility, and to the objectifying effects of the conventions of language; a theory which will *account for* the existence of moral concepts and judgements as they are ordinarily used. A theory of this kind is largely a genetic theory, not an analysis of meaning.[1]

The mental experience to which ethical language is related, of course includes feeling. Moral judgement certainly involves feelings of approval or disapproval, and would not exist if men were not sympathetic. But it is not wholly a matter of feeling, nor, for that matter, are approval and sympathy themselves mere affective states and no more. That sympathy involves imaginative cognition we have tried to show in the previous chapter. As for approval, it is a common objection to emotive theories of ethics that the 'feeling' upon which they

[1]Mr. P. F. Strawson's article 'Ethical Intuitionism' (*Philosophy*, January, 1949) reaches conclusions somewhat similar to those expressed here, particularly when he points out (p. 32) that a naturalistic theory should not be regarded as giving a translation of ethical terms.

usually rely is one which presupposes a thought of rightness or goodness.[1] When we approve of an act, we should usually be willing to say that we approve of it because we think it right. Approval is not a simple, 'groundless' feeling, but a complicated 'sentiment'. It is not a feeling that just occurs independently of thought, like my feeling sick when I see blood although I think the reaction is silly. Like many so-called feelings, approval differs from a simple reaction in the sort of way in which a desire differs from a simple impulse. It is a feeling worked up by and in thought.

But to recognize this is not necessarily to admit non-natural entities. The debate between the advocates of reason and the advocates of feeling in ethics is of little significance. It does not settle the issue between naturalism and non-naturalism. To admit that moral judgements are rational provides neither a bulwark for the rationalist doctrine of the synthetic *a priori* nor 'an insuperable objection to a radical empiricist thesis'.

In this discussion I have indicated my inclination to accept the view of empiricists that the necessity of mathematical propositions is hypothetical, depending either on the definitions of the concepts employed or on deduction from postulates which, if they cannot themselves be proved, should not be taken as necessarily true. But I am not altogether convinced of this thesis. It seems to me that the logical empiricists' account of arithmetic, as built up purely from definitions, is quite convincing. The existence of alternative systems of geometry to the Euclidean system renders at least doubtful the traditional view that the axioms of Euclidean geometry are intuitively self-evident, but I am not sure that the traditional view on this point has been conclusively refuted. It may be, as I think some rationalists would hold, that non-Euclidean geometries presuppose Euclidean, and in that event the thesis that Euclid's axioms involve intuition may still be able to stand. I am not convinced that *all* necessary propositions are the result of definition or deduction from mere postulates. I

[1]Cf. Ross, *Foundations of Ethics*, p. 23; and similarly Reid (in criticism of Hume), *Essays on the Active Powers of Man*, essay v, ch. 7.

still find puzzling, for example, the familiar instances of necessary propositions about colours, and it may be that the necessity of these is not purely formal. Throughout my discussion I have confined the comparison between moral principles and logically necessary propositions to a comparison with mathematics. The logical empiricists' account of mathematics has at least explained the necessities of arithmetic and suggested a possible explanation of the necessities of geometry. Their method has proved useful in some fields and may therefore be tried out in others.

A naturalistic theory of moral judgement is a hypothesis and no more. If a naturalistic theory can do the job it sets out to do, of explaining moral concepts instead of leaving them unexplained, it is to be preferred. The principal reason for seeking such an explanation is the desire for economy, exemplified in Occam's razor. This desire is due to the metaphysical aim of synthesis or unity; one world of entities, if possible, not two or several. Metaphysical thinking is responsible for naturalism as much as for non-naturalism. The more economical view is preferable provided that it is equally able to cover all the phenomena. Whether it does so for geometry is to be determined by examining geometry, and whether it does so for moral judgement is to be determined by examining moral judgement. One of the relevant phenomena is that both mathematical and moral judgement involve the use of 'reason', but this can be equally covered by either of the two metaphysical views. Just as the rationality of Euclid's geometry neither proves nor disproves the real existence of Euclidean space and necessary truths about it, so the rationality of moral judgement neither proves nor disproves the real existence of ethical characteristics and principles.

IX

POLICIES OF CONDUCT

§1. *The humanist ethic and its alternatives*

If my interpretation of morality as we understand it is correct, its leading concern is to ascribe value to persons. The value attaches to them both as individuals and as members of community. As bearers of moral personality they are neither completely distinct from each other nor yet merged into some all-absorbing whole. The emphasis placed on the claims of justice and liberty shows that individuals retain their individuality, and that this has an important place in the moral system. As Martin Buber puts it, morality arises 'between man and man'. It cannot arise within a solitary individual, nor yet does it wipe out the individuality of different men; it lies in their relationship, in inter-personal ties. It also involves treating other individuals equally as ends-in-themselves—equally, because there can be no grading of persons, 'ends-in-themselves', as more or less valuable; degrees of value are determined by the purposes of persons, and so can apply only to *their* ends and derivatively to means thereto. Treating persons as ends-in-themselves thus includes three main points, (*a*) that their individual ends are to be respected, (*b*) that they are members of a community of ends-in-themselves, and (*c*) that they are to be rated equally as ends-in-themselves. These three points are summed up in the slogan 'Liberty, Equality, Fraternity', which is often regarded as putting in a nutshell 'the democratic ethic'.

Could there be alternative policies of action? (1) The most obvious alternative, which has figured prominently in the writings of moral philosophers, is a policy of egoism. To adopt the policy of treating other persons as ends-in-themselves does not imply the rejection of a policy of self-interest. The prescription that we act towards the ends of others as if they were our own ends presupposes the existence and continuance of a general tendency to pursue our own happiness, and this has a place in the moral system as a principle of fitting action and in the claim to liberty. The egoist is one who refuses to *add* the policy of altruism to that of self-love. He accepts the claim of liberty for himself, but does not accept in addition duties to others. He confines himself to a partial acceptance of point (*a*), in the sense that each man, or at least he himself, is entitled to pursue his own happiness.

(2) A second alternative would be to confine oneself to point (*b*), duty to the community as a whole. There could be an ethic devoted simply to the idea of community, regarding the total community of persons as a supra-personal entity to which alone intrinsic value was ascribed. The value of individuals would then be purely instrumental, and the private ends of individuals would be promoted or sacrificed simply in accordance with their instrumental value or disvalue for the social body taken as a whole.

(3) A third alternative policy would deny point (*c*), and would hold that different individuals were unequal in intrinsic worth and not merely in their instrumental value. They should be treated in accordance with their different worths. Only the best men should be considered as ends-in-themselves. The others should be considered as ends in but a limited sense, analogous to that applied to animals. To be sure, they are superior to animals, but the best men are superior to them. As with animals, their ends should be considered when they do not conflict with those of their betters, but when they do they are to be sacrificed without compunction. The ends of the superior group constitute the standard by reference to which instrumental value is rated, and these alone have absolute value.

In practice, it would seem that alternative codes of conduct are less widely prevalent than is often supposed. Professor M. Ginsberg, in his book *Reason and Unreason in Society*,[1] says:

'Contrary to widely held views, comparative studies reveal

[1] pp. 25-6; cf. pp. 303 ff.

> a considerable uniformity in the moral judgments regarding the fundamental social relationships. If we compare the list of *prima facie* duties drawn up by W. D. Ross with the duties enumerated in comparative studies such as Westermarck's, the resemblance is striking. . . . Westermarck himself concludes that "when we study the moral rules laid down by the customs of savage peoples we find that they in a very large measure resemble the rules of civilized nations."
>
> 'The chief difference lies, of course, in the range of persons to whom the rules are held to be applicable, a range which has expanded in the course of history with the expansion of the social units and the accompanying widening of the altruistic sentiments.'

The final sentence of this quotation implies that the third of our alternative creeds is common enough. The first (with which sociologists would in any event not be concerned, since it is a personal and not a social code) and the second are philosophical caricatures. They depict policies which confine themselves to one principle of conduct. What may be found in practice is an *emphasis* upon that one principle. Still, philosophical caricatures can serve a useful purpose in showing up distinctions sharply.

Both in philosophical doctrine and in practice all three possibilities can be found, at least in modified form. (1) There is the morality of Samuel Smiles, self-help. Each for himself and devil take the hindmost. There is also the philosophical view that self-realization is the sole ideal, but as propounded by idealist philosophers this turns into the view that the ideal self to be realized is not the individual self but the Absolute, and then the doctrine is virtually the same as the second alternative, to which we now come. (2) There is the mystical view, common especially in the East, that the individual is to merge himself into some all-embracing spirit. On a more material plane there are collectivist doctrines, which assert that the good of the social whole is alone what matters, the good of the individual having value only as contributing to the former. (3) There are the doctrines of aristocracy, nationalism, and Fascism, according to which a particular group alone is regarded as having full worth or full claims, while the rest are of lesser account to be used as means if their ends conflict with the ends of the superior group. This view is not simply a form of (1), i.e., it is not a policy of individual prudence combined with the realization that no-one is strong enough to be successful in pursuing only his own ends. The egoistic policy may require a man to co-operate with others in the pursuit of their joint ends, but he still does not treat the others as ends-in-themselves. The first view is that of Thrasymachus and Hobbes, the third is that of Plato and Nietzsche. According to the first view, the value of any individuals other than oneself is instrumental; according to the third, the value of some (but not all) individuals other than oneself is intrinsic.

There could be other possibilities too. Each of the policies so far mentioned involves setting up an ideal, and a rule for achieving a harmony of some kind, even if it be only the harmony of the agent's own desires which requires the stifling of some for the sake of others. It is, however, possible to follow a philosophy of *carpe diem,* of yielding to each impulse as it comes. Such a policy might be restricted to egoistic impulses, or it might include all impulses, egoistic and altruistic, or conceivably it might be limited to altruistic impulses alone (far-fetched as that logical possibility is). But nobody acts consistently from impulse, though some people come a little nearer than others to such a life. (Dmitri Karamazov in Dostoevsky's novel lives like this for a good part of his time.) A life that was consistently of this kind would not be human existence at all. It is, we are pleased to suppose, the life of animals, who are mercifully supplied with instinctive tendencies guiding many of their impulses into the direction that a rule of self-preservation would dictate. But even animals, I should imagine, can get a little beyond the stage of being entirely subject to passing impulse. However that may be, when we talk of an *ethic,* we mean a rule or principle of action, a policy implying some sort of deliberate harmonization, and something that is human. So we may neglect these other possibilities and confine our attention to the three previously outlined.

Each of these has its own logic, its own system of rules of conduct, its own way of life; and each has been followed by large groups of men. It is easy to say that an alternative policy to our own is not what is meant by morality. It is not what most members of our society mean by morality, but it may be what other people mean or have meant by morality or the best way of life. Plato's idea of the good life is not the Biblical one. Nor are alternative creeds confined to works of the imagination. Indian mysticism may seem to us both uncongenial and impractical, but it is accepted by large numbers of people in the East and even by some members of our own society who, on comparing it with the ethic of our civilization, think it preferable. For that matter, Spinoza's powerful arguments for submission to the cosmic whole as it is, for an ethic of resignation and absorption in the contemplative love of the universe (which he calls God), as opposed to an ethic of struggle to change and (as we think) improve, is not so very different from the Eastern ethic. A holistic creed, however, need not necessarily be one of resignation and submission. Communism advocates care for the social whole only, but involving an active struggle to improve; and Communism is certainly a real enough alternative to our ethic. So is Nietzschean Fascism or some other doctrine of supermen. As to Samuel Smiles, few of us can have known no moments when we wondered if this was not the sensible way to live; hence the prevalence of egoistic theories in the history of moral philosophy, and the common belief that the end of life is to seek one's own happiness. Again, some aspects of nineteenth-century Liberalism, especially its economic theories, assumed this view (though with a benevolent 'hidden hand' producing a natural harmony between private interests).

It will be noted that I have illustrated the reality of each of these views by pointing, not merely to philosophical theories and personal attitudes to life, but also to political doctrines.

Likewise, the view that we have previously been occupied in analysing, would often be called the 'democratic ethic' or the 'democratic ideal', summed up in the popular slogan of the French Revolutionaries, a political ideal nurtured by Locke and Rousseau (who, however, also has his addiction to the collectivist doctrine), and reaching its deepest and best philosophical formulation in Kant. An ethic, or moral ideal, usually includes a social or political ideal.

At this point we must make a distinction of political theory. It is one thing to hold a 'democratic', an 'aristocratic', or a 'communistic' ethic or ideal; it is another thing to advocate democratic, aristocratic, or communistic government. In one sense, an 'aristocrat' is a person with a certain system of values; e.g., we may mean, in calling him by that name, that he holds some men to be intrinsically superior to others. In another sense, an 'aristocrat' is a man who holds that, whatever ideal we wish to pursue, we shall pursue it best in political affairs by entrusting the conduct of those affairs to people who are in some way best equipped for that task, without necessarily implying that those men are in all respects, or in some fundamental intrinsic respect, superior to the others.

Again, a person who holds that the ideal of life is for the individual to be merged into some greater whole, by no means necessarily thinks that the way to achieve this is by what might be called communistic government, i.e., everyone taking part together in government. In point of fact, Communism is generally understood, not so much as a system of government, but as a doctrine concerning property; it is the doctrine that property which can be directly enjoyed should be distributed according to needs, while property whose value is instrumental should be communally owned. As to systems of government, the Soviet system, like Plato's, is far from giving all members of the society participation in it.

So, too, 'democracy' is ambiguous. People speak of the democratic ideal, meaning the principles of liberty, equality, and fraternity. But more properly, democracy is a form of government, that form which I just now misleadingly called 'communistic' government, i.e., government in which every citizen takes part. Since, in practice, democratic government involves following the decisions of the majority, it is possible for democratic government to pursue ideals other than those sometimes called 'democratic'; for instance, democratic government may lead to a tyranny of the majority, and especially to depressing some manifestations of liberty in the interests of uniformity, as Mill saw in his essay *On Liberty*. Again, it is at least theoretically possible for the ideals of liberty, equality, and fraternity, to be pursued through aristocratic forms of government. The history of government in Europe may make us feel that this theoretical possibility is psychologically impossible, since 'power tends to corrupt'. Yet I found that in the Dutch colony of Curaçao, where the government (so I was told) is frankly authoritarian, the inhabitants, coloured West Indians no less than the Dutchmen, enjoyed a remarkably high measure of prosperity, happiness, and freedom, with apparently complete social equality between the two groups. And a colleague of mine in New Zealand who had spent some years in Burma, affirmed that, in his experience, Acton's aphorism did not by any means always hold good in the East. However, whether or not non-democratic government may in practice co-exist with pursuit of the so-called democratic ideals, it is clear that there is no logically necessary connexion between them. One may certainly hold 'democratic ideals' without thereby thinking that the form of democratic government which we have should be applied *now* to all men. To hold that all men are potentially capable of being moral agents in a universal human community, does not imply that we think all have reached the same level of development now. One may well support tutelary government as an interim measure for less well developed peoples, while being a democrat. This looks like advocating democracy at home, and aristocracy (or Nietzschean views) abroad. In fact, however, it is to regard the backward people as being, in their political capacity, like children who will one day be adult and capable of governing themselves, and who are to be helped forward in their development to that stage. Aristocracy or the Nietzschean view treats the ruled as *permanently* inferior and as means to the interests of the rulers instead of as ends-in-themselves. Of course, Victorian imperialism tended to take this view of colonial peoples, and even now it would be silly to pretend that colonial rule does not aim partly at benefiting the ruling power as well as at enabling the ruled to develop themselves. But in so far as colonial government is true to the democratic ideal, it tends more to the second aim.

We are concerned here with ethical ideals and not forms of government. Words like 'democratic' and 'aristocratic' are, at least etymologically, more appropriate for the description of forms of government. I shall therefore use different adjectives to describe the 'democratic', 'aristocratic', and 'communistic' ideals. I shall call the first the Humanist ethic, as being the view that all men are to count as ends; the second I shall term the Optimate ethic, as being the view that the best men only are to count fully as ends; and the third I shall name the Collectivist ethic, as being the view that the good of the collective whole, and not that of its individual members, is the end to be promoted. In addition to these three, there is the Egoistic ethic.

§2. *The problem of comparing alternative policies*

Is there any rational method of comparing these four policies, any mode of argument which might be used to persuade an adherent of one creed to transfer his allegiance to another? The practical importance of seeking such an argument is not primarily to persuade others, however, for we all know how small is the effect of rational argument in such a debate. But there would be much satisfaction in an ability to justify to ourselves by a rational procedure our adherence to the humanist ethic.

The difficulty is to find a commonly accepted set of relevant premisses from which we may debate the respective merits of the alternative policies. Much of traditional moral philosophy has been concerned with the question why a policy of altruism should be added to that of egoism. The question is asked from the standpoint of the egoist, and therefore the answer also has to be given from that standpoint. To reply that altruism is a duty or has a value of its own is to beg the question at issue. Accordingly, many moral philosophers from Plato onwards have tried to show that virtue pays the best dividends. The answer seems unsatisfactory, not only because we may doubt its truth, but also because it is not a justification of altruism proper. It justifies beneficence to others as a means to our own ends, but does not justify it as an end in itself. Any justification of a course of action presupposes the acceptance of some scale of value, just as any proof of a proposition in theoretical argument presupposes the acceptance of some premisses. In order to persuade an egoist of the merits of altruism, we must base the argument on the scale of value which he accepts. But our purpose is to persuade him to alter his scale of value itself. Is there any common ground which we both accept and from which an argument about the alternative policies of action can proceed?

Most naturalists, I think, would say that there is no such common ground. The adoption of ultimate ends or policies is a matter of feeling or convention. From causes such as these one group has come to espouse one way of life, another a different way, and there can be no question of *rational* dispute about the relative merits of the alternative policies. For a dispute about merits would presuppose a standard of value from which to argue, and it is the ultimate standards of value themselves that we are vainly trying to compare.

A simple naturalistic theory, which says that standards are just expressions of feeling or just conventions, is quite implausible. Feeling is a necessary, but not a sufficient, condition for the emergence of a policy of action. It does not account for the rational character of a standard as a deliberately adopted policy to be applied consistently to all situations irrespective of the varying strength of feelings in different circumstances. The other suggestion of naturalism, convention, is no doubt intended to explain how individuals, growing up in a society with established standards, come to accept and continue those standards. Many individuals, in accepting current standards, do simply regard them as the common form demanded by law or public opinion, and fall in with them either from the herd-like inclination to follow the crowd or from fear of legal and social sanctions. But this does not explain how an individual may come to query current standards and then accept some or reject others by what seems to him a rational judgement. The rationality of his judgement may be accommodated within a naturalistic theory, as we suggested in the last chapter, provided the judgement relates to subordinate principles falling, or failing to fall, under the ultimate 'postulate' of the code. The 'postulate' itself, however, is often regarded, by individuals who think about it, as commendable or otherwise. They may, for instance, judge a maxim of 'love thy neighbour' to be superior to a maxim of self-love.

A more complex theory, combining and adding to the two suggestions of feeling and convention, might take us farther. The 'rationality' of a policy, as being a resolution to act always in one direction so far as possible, might be put down to a desire for consistency, or a dislike of frequent change, inherent in human nature; and the selection of one set of feelings, rather than another, for consistent application, might be put down to the generally prevailing strength of such feelings in those who first preach a particular ethical doctrine. Their preaching will appeal at first only to hearers in whom such feelings are similarly predominant. But once a group of disciples has been formed, a tradition or convention grows up which is strong enough to ensure the conformity of new members born within the group, even though the feeling behind the code may not be the predominant feeling of those new members. When an individual who has been reared in an accepted tradition rejects it, this is because his predominant feelings are at variance with those of the code and are sufficiently strong to overcome the force of convention.

A naturalistic theory of judgement, as we have said before, is a genetic theory. It does not, or rather it should not, pretend to give an analysis of the judgement as that appears to the person making it. A naturalist need not assert that the causes which he alleges for the growth of moral judgement are present to the mind of an agent employing such judgement. The intuitionist describes the way in which the judgement appears to the person using it. When we perceive material things, their colours appear as parts of the objects we see. A causal explanation of how we come to see colours does not entail that in perception we are conscious of the causes of colours. If we wish to give a causal explanation of how men come to accept a particular ethic, the naturalistic theory sketched in the preceding paragraph seems plausible enough. But it does not give us a criterion for the *choice* of an ethic. It seeks to give a deterministic account of how men *have* made such a 'choice'. It gives no help to an agent deliberating which choice he should now make, or seeking a rational justification for the choice he has made. Holders of naturalistic theories of ethics would usually say that they have provided all that can be provided by way of a rational account. One can explain a choice, but not justify it. It has causes but not grounds.

Now the intuitionist agrees that the choice of one policy of action in preference to others, as the right or the best one, cannot be justified by extraneous reasons. But he does not agree that the choice must therefore be non-rational. He would say that it should be guided by self-evidence. The principle which it is right to adopt is self-evidently so, a synthetic *a priori* truth. If a supporter of a different ethical system, resting on a different set of ultimate principles, claims that to him our principles are not self-evident and his own are, there is nothing for it but to declare that he is morally blind.

The metaphor, however, uses the analogy of sense-perception, in which we know from experience that men differ. 'Reason' is supposed to be universally the same, independent of the vagaries of bodily organs, and this is one of the grounds for the view that reason discloses the real nature of things. A man may be incapable of solving a problem in higher mathematics; if so, he would not claim to know the answer. But if a man gave an alternative answer to the correct one, and claimed that he had reasoned it out, we should be able to show him mistakes in his reasoning. This analogy is not a fair one, because the rationalist in ethics is referring to intuition and not reasoning. But if we take non-ethical examples of what he would claim to be intuited truths, e.g., simple mathematical propositions, we do not find a close analogy. A child may be incapable of seeing that four times five must equal twenty, but we do not find him asserting stoutly that he sees an alternative answer to be necessary. His intellectual 'blindness' is like the blindness of a puppy and not like colour-blindness. If we turn instead to the ultimate axioms of mathematics and logic, non-rationalists may deny that they have an intuition of synthetic *a priori* truth, and the rationalist may call them blind; but they do not claim to intuit alternative axioms.

Both views, naturalist and rationalist alike, imply a *non disputandum* about ultimate ethical principles or ends. The naturalists say this is because our ethical policy has causes but no grounds; it is just the result of the way we happen to be constituted or to have been brought up. The rationalists say it is because we can only 'look' and 'see'—or, if we are 'blind', fail to 'see'. It may be that one must in the end fall back to one or other of these views, but both have their difficulties. The naturalist view fails to explain how changes of policy sometimes seem to involve a rational judgement, and the rationalist view fails to account for the positive assertion of alternative policies by different groups of men. Before accepting their common conclusion that no argument is possible about ultimate principles, we should consider what methods of comparing alternative policies might be suggested.

An appeal to our subjective preferences, or to the ordinary moral judgements of our society, will of course not do. It is simply a form of the naturalist's scepticism. The advocates of opposing policies can equally cite their preferences and the moral judgements of those who agree with them. We are not appealing to anything that is common ground between the two parties.

An appeal to religion meets with a similar difficulty. If our opponents hold a different religious belief, which supports their ethical creed to the extent that our religious belief supports our ethical creed, we are faced with the task of proving that our religion is true and theirs false. Any ethical creed can be supported by, or stated in the form of, a religious belief, and the problem of comparing ethical creeds is simply translated into different language if we decide instead to compare different religious beliefs.

Can we appeal instead to human nature? Bishop Butler argued that 'your obligation to obey this law is its being the law of your nature'.[1] But then he seems to presuppose that every man's conscience dictates the same policy of action, and this is not true unless we decide arbitrarily to say that what a Hitler thinks right is not the dictate of his conscience. Still, one might argue along Butlerian lines that the alternative policies to the humanist ethic fail to take account of all the elements of human nature. It will have been noticed that, before looking around at the different ethical creeds in the world, I produced the three alternative policies theoretically from the humanist ethic by selecting or rejecting one or other part of the latter. The egoistic view selects and confines itself to a limited part of the principle of individuality, affirming the right of each individual to pursue his own ends but nothing more. The collectivist view confines itself to the principle of community. The optimate view was derived, not by picking out and affirming a single element in the humanist policy, but by denying one such element, namely the principle of equality. But then what the optimate view comes to is the affirmation that *some* men are ends-in-themselves, and that others are (relatively) means to the former. It thus may be said to recognize, but with more limited scope, one part of the humanist creed, for the latter likewise ascribes intrinsic value to a class of beings but extends the class to include all men as opposed to other creatures, while the optimate view ascribes such value to one class of men as opposed to others. The humanist creed

[1]Sermon iii.

is, therefore, more comprehensive than the others. It includes each of the alternative policies, and extends the scope of the egoistic and optimate policies so as to make a coherent as well as a comprehensive system. Now each of the limited alternative policies is plainly connected with a prominent factor in human nature. Can we say that the humanist policy is preferable in that it does justice to *all* factors in precarious balance?

This suggestion, however, will not convince the adherents of the other creeds. They will not agree that it is right to make room for all natural tendencies. The argument relies on the basic imperative, 'Give effect to all factors in human nature', and the opposing creeds may reject that policy as much as the principles which are alleged to flow from it. An egoist may say: 'It it is true that compassion and the gregarious instinct often lead us to neglect our individual interests, but it is weakness and folly to allow these to deflect us from our own interest'. An upholder of the optimate view will tell us that it is foolish and wrong to be deflected from the valuing of quality in human beings. A collectivist will think it wrong to be deflected, by selfishness or compassion for individuals, from the pursuit of the good of the community as a whole.

Even if it could be taken for granted that there will be common acceptance of the claims of all motives natural to man, this does not necessarily lead to the humanist ethic. For an ethic, or policy of life, presupposes some measure of free choice and includes a determination to act at times in ways that are contrary to the line of least resistance. In most men egoistic motives are stronger than altruistic, and morality as we understand it in the humanist tradition frequently involves an effort to be altruistic where our strongest natural inclination is to be egoistic. The humanist creed does not simply cater for all factors of human nature, leaving the preponderance, in cases of conflict, to the natural strength of the conflicting motives. Some allowance is made for egoism, but frequently the policy goes against 'human nature' in recommending that a naturally weak altruism should be espoused instead of a naturally strong egoism. A policy of action involves choice, and it is this which has to be justified. A life which merely followed 'human nature' all the time would be determined, not chosen, and no question of justification would arise. Bishop Butler's appeal was to an *ideal* of human nature, as he well knew, to 'human nature' as he thought it ought to be. He ascribes to certain factors in human nature a 'superiority' or 'authority' which is independent of their 'strength' in human nature as it is. In my opinion, Butler's appeal to the 'superiority' or 'authority' of conscience rests on theological doctrine.[1] But in any event, reference to an ideal of human nature goes beyond positive psychology.

All attempts to make a *direct* comparison between alternative policies of life must rest on presupposed judgements of value, which are themselves the subject of debate. There can therefore be no commonly accepted premisses from which to argue. It seems to me that the only possible method of argument is an *indirect* one, of eliminating alternatives on their own ground. We might take each policy by itself, accepting its own premisses for the sake of argument, and see if it can be realized in practice. There are two ways in which it might fail to do so. First, we might find that human beings could not in fact use the policy as a guide to action. Secondly, a policy that could be pursued might lead to results inconsistent with its own aim. Even in the second case we could conclude that the proposed policy was not a practicable way of life; it would be self-stultifying, or 'pragmatically self-contradictory', in a manner analogous to the self-contradiction inherent in an inconsistent system of theoretical belief. The first test assumes, as a commonly accepted premiss, the principle that a policy of life must permit of being pursued; the second assumes common acceptance of the principle that a policy of life must permit of consistent realization, just as debate on theoretical issues presupposes a common repudiation of self-contradiction. We are certainly justified in assuming acceptance of the first premiss,

[1]Cf. my article 'Bishop Butler's View of Conscience', published in *Philosophy*, July, 1949.

for it is presupposed by the idea of a policy or guide to action. And I think we are justified in postulating the second, on the ground that a policy or principle is intended to be a rational guide for life as a whole. The 'rationality' of a policy lies partly in its fitting the facts of life, and partly in the determination to pursue it consistently, thereby presupposing the possibility of consistent pursuit and of success in achieving the chosen end by means of such pursuit.

Let us therefore apply these tests to the alternative policies we have listed. To do so, our appeal must be empirical. The egoistic policy can be put into practice, but it fails the second test. There is a familiar objection to egoism, which I think is supported by reasonably good evidence, that to aim at happiness is to miss it. A man who simply keeps his eye on the pursuit of his own happiness is apt to find, at the end of his life, that he has not attained his ideal and might have come nearer to it if he had not pursued it directly.

I have already suggested in Chapter V, §4, that the optimate policy cannot be put into practice. And what is practicable soon meets the second hurdle. When we discussed the claim to equality, we agreed that men are unequal in 'worth' if that be taken to refer to natural endowments or moral achievement. The optimate policy wishes to pick out one or more of these qualities and to regard as fully ends-in-themselves only those men who come up to a high degree of worth in respect of such qualities. But in practice it is impossible to conduct our dealings with men so as to conform to their actual inequalities. It is, of course, possible to treat one group of men as superior to the rest, but it is not practicable to do so in accordance with natural 'worth'. Plato's hope of being able to pick out the golden and silver citizens at the start, and keep them in separate groups, is a vain dream. Any attempt to base society on natural inequalities is bound to cut across or exceed the inequalities of nature, and so give rise to protest and revolution. The practical implication of this is not that things must always be left as they are with no attention paid to the different worths of different men. We may find by experience as we go along that it is socially *useful* to provide some particular good for John Smith; e.g., to give him facilities for the exercise of certain endowments which we find he possesses and which will be beneficial to society. But we cannot decide *a priori* that all the John Smiths have useful capacities, still less that they are superior in some more absolute sense. The optimate view, which wishes to distinguish differences of intrinsic worth, is impracticable; and since the attempt to follow it merely leads to a struggle in which the stronger come out as victors, it is 'pragmatically self-contradictory' unless its criterion of excellence at the start is that of strength. If an optimate doctrine is based on power, and not on some other qualities as constituting human excellence, I do not think we can argue against it. It is a doctrine resting on force and not on reason, and therefore does not admit of rational argument. Undoubtedly such a view just has to be met on its own terms of power. While the practical force of this is only too obvious, it does not remove our problem, which is that of a rational justification of one policy as against others. A man who seeks such a justification is committed to rational procedures and has rejected the appeal to force.

The collectivist view seems to fail the first test on psychological grounds. It is surely impossible for at any rate most individuals to forget their individuality and act simply as part of a greater whole. Psychological studies of crowds suggest that there are occasions when individuality is at a minimum, but what is then observed is wholly determined behaviour and not deliberate, self-determining action. The collectivist creed seems to refer to an unattainable ideal, one that is held in view in order to enable individuals to think a little less of themselves than they naturally would, and a little more of others. It is, so to say, the high-lighting of one element in morality, an element which, owing to human selfishness, it is difficult to aim at. So regarded, the collectivist ethic is a part of the humanist. But if taken as a self-sufficient policy prescribing an attainable end, it seems quite unsuited to the practical life.

Our pragmatic arguments have shown weaknesses in the

alternatives to the humanist ethic, but it would be a mistake to think that the latter is left unaffected. For although it can be put into practice, it is liable to result in a kind of pragmatic inconsistency. If we are to treat all men as ends-in-themselves, what are we to do when different persons whom we can affect by our action have conflicting ends? In a conflict of obligations, we often have to neglect the obligation to treat one person, or one group of persons, as an end or ends. The problem comes out with particular poignancy in the dilemma of war. Taking part, and refusing to take part, in what one acknowledges to be a just war, both involve a failure to treat some men as ends-in-themselves. To kill is to fail to treat as ends those whom we kill. To stand aside is to fail to treat as ends those people who are being oppressed, or are threatened with oppression, by the aggressors. We must decide where we think the balance of obligation lies, but we cannot escape the fact that the universality of the humanist ethic is at times impracticable. In such dilemmas the humanist has to adopt, for the moment, one variety of the optimate policy. He has to choose the ends of those whom he considers to have the superior moral cause. But he does so for the moment only, and looks forward to the time when he can again treat as ends-in-themselves those whom he now treats as means. Unlike the optimate creed, his ethic does not allow him to regard them as having no claim upon him. We can say, as we said before, that the necessity of the moment to prefer the ends of one group does not justify a permanent preference of that group, because the difference between the two groups is not, like the difference between men and animals, permanent and permanently obvious.

I do not think that these pragmatic considerations give us a conclusive argument for preferring the humanist ethic. It seems to me that the humanist ethic comes out of the discussion a little better than any of its rivals, but the matter needs fuller and closer argument than I have been able to give it. One cannot help feeling, however, that a pragmatic test is really beside the point. The initial appeal of an ethical doctrine does not seem to owe anything to the thought that it will work successfully. When one is impressed by some parts of Biblical doctrine, and feels that they reach a 'higher' standard than had been reached before, they often seem far from practical. One seems therefore to be driven back in the end to the view of both the intuitionist and the naturalist that there is no room for rational argument in the adoption of an ultimate policy of action.

We saw that both these views had their difficulties. But our discussion of possible methods of comparing alternative policies now allows us to mitigate our former objections. (1) Our objection to intuitionism was this. Analogies with perception and the self-evidence of mathematics and logic should imply the absence of 'vision' in the 'blind' and not the illusory 'seeing' of alternatives. We have now noticed, however, especially in our discussion of the proposed appeal to human nature, that the alternative policies to the humanist are not fully opposed alternatives but are partial selections from the humanist ethic. If so, the adherents of these alternative policies may be like colour-blind men who see some colours but not all, or like men of average intelligence who can proceed some way in mathematics but not so far as the mathematically gifted. (2) Our objection to naturalism was that, while it explained *how* men have come to adopt one policy rather than another, it denied any possibility of justifying such a choice. We may now say, on behalf of the naturalist, that the initial appeal of a policy lies in the force of tradition or of the predominant feelings of the individual, but a method of justification may be found in the practical results of alternative choices.

My discussion of this topic has been cursory and inconclusive. I do not feel able at present to give a wholly convincing justification of the humanist ethic; and I cannot make up my mind whether to adopt, in the final analysis, the position of the naturalist or that of the intuitionist. I think that the existence of alternative ethical policies deserves more discussion than it has received from moral philosophers, both for its bearing on the political problem of conflicting ideologies and for its relevance to the metaphysical problems of ethical theory.

X

ETHICS AND SCIENCE: THE PROBLEM OF FREE WILL

§1. *Apparent conflicts between ethics and other fields of thought*

Our last task in the metaphysic of morals is to consider whether the presuppositions of moral judgement conflict with those of any other established body of knowledge or belief. Here the main problem is that of free will *versus* determinism, an apparent clash between ethics and science. Moral judgement appears to presuppose free will, and science appears to presuppose determinism. Since the sciences are, for the most part, an established body of knowledge accepted by all, ethics must meet the challenge that it seems to contradict an axiom of science.

There are also apparent conflicts between ethics and orthodox theology. One of these likewise concerns free will. The doctrine of divine omniscience, if this includes knowledge of the future, seems at first sight to have implications inconsistent with freedom of human choice, though it may not be too difficult to show that there is no real inconsistency here. The doctrine of predestination undoubtedly conflicts with free will, but predestination seems to me unacceptable on purely theological grounds anyway. The second possible conflict between ethics and theology concerns the problem of evil. Moral thinking proceeds on the assumption that there is evil to be overcome, while Biblical theology tells us that God is both omnipotent and perfectly good, so that his creation must be the best of all possible worlds. Here, too, there may be no genuine conflict. If the theologian takes his doctrine to imply that evil is unreal, his conclusion does clash with the moral thinking of common sense. A naturalistic interpretation of ethical terms will not make this any the less true, for the 'goodness' of God will still refer to his benevolence, among other attributes, and we shall still have the problem of explaining how a benevolent and omnipotent God can cause misery for the objects of his benevolence. On the other hand, if the theologian accepts the reality of evil and tries to show that it is a necessary condition for securing the best of all possible worlds, this may be quite consistent with the implications of ethics.

The resolution of these problems is a matter for the metaphysic of theology rather than the metaphysic of morals. For first, they are also problems for the logic of theology, i.e., for the internal consistency of theology itself. Biblical theology includes the doctrine that God endowed man with free will, no less than the doctrine of divine omniscience. And the theological problem of evil primarily concerns the relation between the divine attributes of omnipotence and perfect goodness. Secondly, in so far as the problem of evil is a conflict between a theoretically consistent theology and the common-sense evaluation of good and evil in the world, the presuppositions giving rise to the problem are those of theology. Ethics takes the world as we find it, including its evil, while orthodox theology postulates a creator who is both omnipotent and wholly good, a doctrine hard to square with the apparent character of his creation. Apart from the doubts of many about the existence of God, a number of believers has always inclined to a Manichaean doctrine, in which God's power is limited. Experience of apparently unjustified evil in the world is one of the chief grounds for religious scepticism and the Manichaean heresy. It is for theologians to show whether the orthodox doctrine can fit the facts.

In the apparent conflict between ethics and science, however, the onus lies on the moral philosopher, at least as much as on the philosopher of science, to examine the presuppositions on each side which seem to clash with each other. While many people feel less sure of their theological than of their ethical beliefs, few would be prepared to jettison an acceptance of natural science rather than the traditional interpretation of ethics if forced to choose between them. I shall try to show that what needs to be jettisoned is the traditional interpretation of science given by the doctrine of determinism.

§2. *Causation and causal laws*

Science, it is generally thought, presupposes determinism and morality presupposes free will. If these presuppositions conflict, we have a fundamental inconsistency between two departments of thought—and not of thought alone, but of thought on which we base action. For obviously we act as if the main body of scientific thought were true, and our lives are deeply affected by it. No less obviously, we act as if our moral conceptions were true, and our lives are deeply affected by them. Now surely, if this be so, there cannot really be a conflict. There might be inconsistency between beliefs one of which did not affect action. We might talk as if we believed one thing and act as if we believed another, so that the inconsistency would be between our profession and our practice, a not unfamiliar situation. But when we act as if we believed what we say, a fundamental inconsistency between two sets of such beliefs would produce a conflict in action—unless the two classes of action affected by the two sets of belief could be kept quite separate from each other, a desperate expedient sometimes adopted but quite impossible to maintain on all occasions.

I do not believe that there is any inconsistency between the freedom required by morals and the presuppositions required by scientific inquiry. The philosophical problem of free will *versus* determinism is generated, I think, by confusion of different senses of the word 'cause'. Let us first try to clear up this confusion.

It has been thought that libertarianism means that acts, or some acts, are uncaused, and that the view denies the universality of the causal axiom, 'Every change has a cause'. Now whether or not we are justified in applying the causal axiom to the whole universe, we must certainly say that the changes involved in deliberate action are caused. At any rate, if the statement that a change is uncaused implies that it happens by chance (as libertarianism, interpreted as the view that voluntary acts are uncaused, is alleged to imply), we plainly cannot accept the conclusion that our deliberate acts happen by chance. If they did, there would be no point in calling them deliberate. Further, this view that voluntary acts are uncaused would be fatal to morals. We could not then impute responsibility, for, on this view, it was purely by chance that the agent did wrong. Again, punishment of the agent would be both unjust and pointless; unjust, because he was not responsible for his wrong act; pointless, because the punishment will not affect his or other people's future action since that, too, will be undetermined and so uninfluenced by anything done to the wrongdoer now. Thus responsibility and the rationale of punishment both require that voluntary acts shall have been caused.

Are we then to accept determinism? We must undoubtedly accept the view that voluntary acts are caused, but determinism means more than this. It is taken to imply that the agent could not have acted otherwise, the antecedents of his act being what they were. This, however, seems preposterous to common sense; it is just incredible to say that I could not, simply of my own volition here and now, choose to alter the next word I shall write after this sentence. Further, the proposed view is, no less than the chance theory, fatal to moral notions. For 'ought' implies 'can', and blame and remorse imply that we could have refrained from an action judged wrong. If, when I have deliberately done wrong, I could not have acted otherwise, it makes no sense to say I *ought* to have refrained, nor can I be blameworthy. Of course, we may say I am 'responsible' for the act in the sense that it was mine and not yours; that is, if redress has to be forthcoming from some quarter, it is sensible to regard me as more concerned than anyone else (just as the law makes me responsible for the acts of my dog). Some determinists think this is a sufficient account of *moral* responsibility, but moral responsibility contains a further idea. If it were the same as this type of responsibility, it would be improper to say of my deliberate wrongful act that I *ought* to have refrained; it would be proper to make only such statements as, 'What a pity the circumstances were not such as to make me refrain', or 'The results would have been better if I refrained'. These are not moral judgements but pointless laments, a childish crying over spilt milk. It will not do to reply that moral judgements *are* really childish. That is just what they are not. Full moral judgements (as opposed to certain types of quasi-moral judgement which may not imply free will) are made by and imputed to adults and not children. If the thoughts expressed by them are fancies, they are fancies confined to adults, not the fancies of children.

It may be argued, however, that the kind of responsibility allowed for on a determinist view is a sufficient account of moral responsibility because the retrospective judgements that it permits are not pointless laments but have their point in their determination of future action. Mr. P. Nowell-Smith (in his article 'Freewill and Moral Responsibility', to which we referred in Chapter V, §2) holds that the language of praise and blame, and the provision of reward and punishment, are still sensible on a determinist theory for their utility in altering future conduct. In his view, 'morally responsible' or 'voluntary' action is action (necessarily) caused by characteristics, the future manifestations of which are alterable by means of praise and blame, reward and punishment. Such action is called morally responsible or voluntary because the force of its motives is liable to be altered by this sort of determinant. The schoolboy who gets his sums wrong from laziness is blamed and punished, not because he could literally have chosen on that occasion to get them right, but because, with that kind of motive for his action, blame and punishment are effective in helping to produce sums worked out correctly next time. For the boy who gets his sums wrong from stupidity, blame and punishment are ineffective towards securing the desired result of correct sums next time. A man who has stolen from cupidity is deterred from future thieving by punishment, a kleptomaniac is not. Therefore we call the actions of the lazy boy and the normal thief 'voluntary' and 'immoral', meaning simply that expressions of disapproval accompanied by the infliction of pain alter, in a desired direction, the future manifestations in action of their dispositions.

Now Mr. Nowell-Smith tells us that if one schoolboy gets his sums wrong from laziness, his teacher achieves the altered result in future by punishing the boy; if another pupil gets his sums wrong from stupidity, the teacher achieves the altered result in future by giving the boy extra tuition. Again, the thief who has stolen from cupidity has his future action altered by punishment, while the kleptomaniac has his altered by psycho-analytic treatment. Then why should we pick out alterability by praise and blame, reward and punishment, from alterability by other means, if the point of praise and blame, reward and punishment, is solely utilitarian, i.e. alteration of future conduct in a desired direction? Alteration by tuition or psycho-analysis, where those are found to be effective, serve the utilitarian purpose just as well. If both types of motive are alterable, why should we call the one moral and immoral, the other not, and why should we call the acts resulting from the one voluntary, from the other involuntary? (It will, of course, not do to say the difference is that in the first type of alterability, by praise and blame, reward and punishment, the alteration results from an internal cause, and in the second type from an external. In each type there is a remote external cause, the acts of other persons, and a proximate internal cause.) Thus Mr. Nowell-Smith's theory does not account for the different language we use.

Further, as we have seen in Chapter V, §2, it does not fit the facts which it is designed to explain, for if we accept the theory we shall have to widen the class of voluntary and morally responsible behaviour far beyond the limits in fact observed in the ordinary use of moral language. According to this theory, any administration of pleasure and pain that helps to cause desired behaviour to continue to be manifested, and undesired behaviour to be altered for the future to desired behaviour, is to be called reward and punishment, and the sort of behaviour so affected is to be called voluntary and moral or immoral. This view, of course, accounts for some of the language used in the training of infants, where people do speak of 'punishment', if not so often of 'reward', though the traditional moralist will say the word 'punishment' is misapplied because infants are not morally responsible. But the theory also implies that carrots and blows for the donkey are to be called reward and punishment, and that the donkey's behaviour is to be called voluntary and moral or immoral.

I conclude that Mr. Nowell-Smith's acutely argued theory is not a satisfactory account of moral responsibility, and that moral responsibility is different from the sort of responsibility allowed by determinism. Moral notions require us to say that deliberate acts are caused, but to deny that they are determined in a sense implying that the agent could not, at that time without alteration of the then existing circumstances, have acted otherwise.

Why is it thought that a man could not have acted otherwise than he did, that determinism in this form is true? Is it a consequence of the causal axiom, 'Every event has a cause'? Surely not, for this principle does not say that a specified set of causes must produce a specified event. It simply says that for there to be *an* event there must be *a* cause. It says nothing about the character of the event. Determinism in its popular form is thought to follow, not from the causal axiom, 'Every event has a cause', but from the supposed assumption of science that all events are subject to *causal laws*, and this is saying, roughly, 'Same cause, same effect'. Now I think the trouble is that the notion of 'cause' here is not analysed. The principle of universal determination, alleged to be assumed by science, says something like this:

(1) Whenever an event of sort *B* occurs, it is always preceded by an event (or set of events) of sort *A*.

(2) Changes are caused by forces, which are always mathematically commensurable (*a*) with each other, and

(*b*) with the change produced. (The inclusion of the words 'caused' and 'produced' in this rough definition of 'causal laws' may seem to involve a vicious circle. The sequel will show that this is not so. 'Cause', as it occurs within the definition, is a different notion from that which appears in the definiendum 'causal law'.) As to (*a*), forces are commensurable with each other in their relative degrees of strength. As to (*b*), a force (or the resultant of a balance of forces) is commensurate in its degree of strength with the amount of change which it produces. For example, two opposing forces of equal strength set up an equilibrium, so that no change occurs, while a force of greater strength than an opposing force produces a change that is somehow correlated mathematically with the degree to which the first force exceeds the second.

All this is taken for granted in classical mechanics, and determinism in moral theory is the transfer to psychology of this principle. But the second part of the principle, the lengthy statement about commensurable forces, hardly makes sense in the psychology of action, and is (as stated above) in any event a piece of metaphysics needing justification. It makes sense to correlate degrees of force (whatever that may be) with amount of movement in space relative to a time interval. The amount of space covered and the interval of time taken to cover it are measurable, and by 'force' is presumably meant something else that is measurable on some sort of scale (e.g., the product of weight and velocity in the object said to exert the force). But it seems dubious to talk of human volitions as if they covered a greater or less amount of something (as of space, though perhaps measurement of a time interval could be relevant). This part of the principle, then, is not applicable to the psychology of action as it is to mechanics. It is also, I said, in any event a piece of metaphysics if taken literally in the form in which I have expressed it. If these 'forces' of which mechanics speaks are not simply shorthand descriptions of what can be observed and measured (e.g., weight and velocity) of the object said to exert the force, they are animistic analogies taken over from the activity which persons exert—as if there were a spirit in the wind, who decides to send hats whirling into the air. I think that, in fact, the 'forces' of mechanics were originally animistic analogies, and were then transformed into shorthand descriptions of what can be observed.

Now if the talk of forces, in our analysis of causal laws, is given the positivist interpretation of being a shorthand description of observable phenomena, as it must be if we are to drop the animistic metaphysics of the other interpretation, then part (2) of our analysis becomes the statement that, in any regular sequence of events (or sets of events) of sort *A* followed by events of sort *B* (the sequences referred to in part (1) of our analysis), certain measurable properties of the events of sort *A* can be correlated with each other and with certain measurable properties of the events of sort *B*. Thus the assumption of determinism in mechanics is simply the view that all events happen in regular sequences, and that any particular pair of events (or of sets of events) falling under any of these sequences can be described and correlated mathematically. In all this there is nothing of *must;* and we have learned from Hume that in causal laws talk of 'necessity' can only be justified as talk of *universality,* of 100% regularity of sequence. Of course, Hume recognizes that this leaves out something in our notion of the necessity of causal sequence. While I think he has shown that this additional something is unjustifiably attributed to the objects involved in the sequence, I do not agree with his account of it. He says that this (as I have said that the original notion of 'force') is an animistic projection. It is, he holds, a projection to the external world of our feeling compelled (being involuntarily *affected)* to expect the second term of the sequence (while I have said that 'force' is a projection of our voluntary *exertion* of activity). Hume's explanation would be a plausible supplement to the account of why we attribute *force* (activity) to *particular* material things; that is, we attribute activity to them because we may be passively affected in their presence, as we may by the activity of other persons. But Hume's view is not a plausible account of the 'necessity' attributed to a *regularity of sequence* among *classes* of material things. I think this notion of 'necessity' is an analogy from logical necessity, and is attributed because the regularity of sequences allows us to make inferences; that is, because we can infer from regular sequences, we think the ground of the (in fact inductive) inference is the same as the ground of deductive inference. Hume's discussion of causation, the merits of which are beyond question, confuses the two senses of cause ('efficient cause' = activity, and 'causal law' = universal regularity of sequence) which I am here trying to disentangle. However, I take Hume to have shown convincingly that the 'necessity' of causal laws can be justifiably interpreted only as meaning universality, i.e. 100% regularity, of sequence.

Causal laws are not the only kind of scientific laws. Causal laws state 100% regularity of temporal sequence. Some of the regularities used for scientific purposes, however, are not universal but refer to a constant, or fairly constant, or regularly changing, proportion of instances of the class of things or events concerned. Others refer, not to temporal sequence, but to some other kind of relation that may vary or be constant. It is perfectly good scientific procedure for an insurance company to bank on 1% of thefts on insured properties in Great Britain during the next year, if there have been, on average, 1% of thefts in recent years, and if there are no discernible relevant differences in the circumstances. Here the actuary uses a regularity (thefts where there is insured property) of less than 100%. Again, it is equally good scientific procedure for a surveyor to bank on discovering tin in Stewart Island, New Zealand, if he knows that the island contains the type of rock, tourmaline granite, which has been invariably, or almost invariably, found to accompany tin ore in other parts of the world. Here the surveyor uses a (100%, or almost 100%) regularity not of temporal sequence but of spatial concomitance. The use of such a regularity does not mean that the granite is thought to cause the existence of tin. It may be said:

'But the universal co-existence of the substances, and the constant though not universal percentage of the thefts, are due to some cause, so that causation does enter into statistical laws of these kinds too'. Say if you will that they are due to some cause, but this is not required, and is irrelevant, for the use made of the regularities observed. Whether the percentage of thefts be attributed to the extent of original sin, or to contemporary conditions in Great Britain, makes no difference to the actuary; he uses the percentage simply, and is unaffected by the theories of theologians and sociologists as to the causes of crime. Whether the co-existence of tourmaline granite and tin be attributed to some occult force of mutual attraction between the two substances, or to the chemical action of volcanic hot waters, makes no difference to the surveyor; he uses the observed co-existence, and is unaffected by the theories of alchemy or of geological history. Of course, some of these theories may state, or imply, more general laws of regularity, and of those, some may be causal laws, i.e. 100% regularities of temporal sequence (this would apply to the theory of volcanic hot waters, if it is true); and the more general laws, including the causal ones, may be used by scientists for other purposes. But for the purpose in hand (computing insurance premiums, or surveying Stewart Island for tin), it is the specific, not the more general, regularity that is used.

It appears, therefore, that scientific procedure involves the use of laws of regularity, preferably reducing them to statistical form so as to assign a fixed mathematical probability, which may be anything from zero to 100%. Laws of *100%* regularity of *temporal sequence*, the so-called 'causal laws', are merely one special (and, of course, very important) class of scientific laws.

Further, the assumption of scientific procedure that all occurrences follow highly and constantly regular patterns, *is* an assumption, it is not known *a priori*. It is an assumption of method. We cannot say that it has worked for all facts, since that would imply that there is nothing left for scientists to investigate or discover. They proceed, however, by seeking such patterns, and certainly experience and results so far suggest a very high degree of regularity in the universe as a whole. But we do not *know* in advance that there is a high degree of regularity everywhere. Events taking place within the spiral nebulae *might* be relatively random, for all we know. We can only find out what sort of regularity there is among events by looking, when and where we can. When we do look, what we in fact seem to find is a higher degree of regularity among some types of events than among others.

'Causal laws' are statements of 100% regularity of temporal sequence. I have said that acts subject to moral predication are 'caused'. What connexion is there between these two uses of the word 'cause'? Precious little, apart from history, and the history is what has given rise to the problem of free will *versus* scientific determinism.

Aristotle, it will be recalled, distinguished four senses of the word 'cause': (1) 'material cause', i.e. the *stuff* of which a thing is made; (2) 'formal cause', the *pattern* according to which it is made; (3) 'efficient cause', what *makes* it to be what it is; (4) 'final cause', the *purpose* or end for which it is made. None of these is the sense of 'cause' employed in the expression 'causal law'. That is a post-Renaissance conception, and consequently the problem of moral freedom in the face of scientific determinism does not appear among the Greeks. Aristotle's discussion of 'incontinence' (ἀκρασία), in the *Nicomachean Ethics,* has nothing to do with the difficulties raised by determinism. His main concern is to explain how (to give a psychological description of what happens when) we fail to do that action which, of actions within our power, we think best. His discussion is not really concerned with the question *whether* we can choose to act one way or the other. True, he considers the matter in relation to the Socratic doctrine that 'incontinence' is impossible, and his final description of what happens, when a man is said to act 'incontinently', seems to involve an acceptance of that doctrine although he says he repudiates it. But the metaphysical doctrine of Socrates which gives rise to Aristotle's problem, is the view that it is impossible to act contrary to one's judgement of what is best. The metaphysical principle underlying the rejection of free will by scientific determinism, is the view that it is impossible to act contrary to the greatest weight of inclination. The modern problem of free will *versus* determinism is entirely due to a particular interpretation of seventeenth-century science. A somewhat similar problem, as we noted, is raised by the theological doctrine of divine foreknowledge, but it is not quite the same. For the theological doctrine is, I suppose, that God has direct precognition of the future, not that he infers the future from his knowledge of the past or of the regular laws governing the universe. Consequently, the problem involved is not raised by predictability from inference, and so differs from the problem for free will raised by the doctrine of scientific determinism (or the popular version of that). At any rate, my concern here is solely with the latter problem.

The idea of a 'causal law' is different from all the four kinds of 'cause' enumerated by Aristotle. Further, neither his 'material' nor his 'formal' nor his 'final' cause is what we mean by the word 'cause' in modern tongues. We do use it in the remaining one of the Aristotelian senses, 'efficient cause', and I think this is the basic meaning of the word. Now where do we get the idea of efficient causation? From our own activity, when we make things, perform actions, initiate change. When we do this, we do it for a purpose, to achieve an end; and we do it by means of making a change in the form of some material. That is to say, where there occurs an instance of efficient causation in human activity, it goes along with the other things mentioned by Aristotle, changing the form of some material for a purpose. That is why Aristotle calls those others things 'causes' in their different senses, for it is primarily with reference to human activity that Aristotle speaks. In all this nothing is implied of laws or of necessity.

Now by analogy, we may conceive of persons like ourselves acting similarly. If we think of the universe as an artefact, we shall be inclined to say (for we have no other analogy) that it was made as we might make something. Some person made it, for a purpose, and the Greeks added that he did so by changing the form of some material. Newton's *Principia,* no less than traditional theology, presupposes, as he recognized in the concluding *Scholium Generale,* a '*rerum omnium fabricator ac dominus*', who is an '*ens intelligens et potens*' having regard to '*causae finales*'; and Newton went on to say explicitly that '*sermo omnis de deo a rebus humanis per similitudinem aliquam desumitur*'. In the same way, I suggest, if we think of *matter* as an efficient cause, exerting activity or 'force', if we really think of this, we can only do so animistically. Later, of course, we may continue to use the *word* 'cause' of matter when the animistic analogy has faded. That stage having been reached in the ordinary connotation, scientists then found that the regular changes in matter could be described mathematically in 'laws', and since men had come to apply the notion of cause to these changes, the scientific 'laws' were called '*causal* laws'. The use of the word 'laws' to describe the regularities is, of course, likewise the ghost (and originally a full-blooded representative) of an analogy from human action. For Newton, a law of motion is a regular principle which God follows in effecting changes in the material world, though Newton does regard '*causae mechanicae*' as exercising '*vis*'. If the reference to God be dropped as too metaphysical for scientific purposes, the notion of 'forcing' must also be dropped as equally metaphysical (analogical), and we are left with 'laws' that are statements of what regularly happens. The notion of efficient causation, i.e. *activity,* has disappeared.

The suggestion that the attribution of force or power to matter was originally animistic is, of course, not new. Among others, Collingwood included this view in his account of the concept of cause in his *Essay on Metaphysics.* He, too, with far more historical knowledge than I possess, distinguished different senses of the word 'cause' and held that the connexion between them must be sought in history. Oddly enough, however, although he drew attention to two senses of the word 'cause' (not directly relevant to my thesis) that are different from the sense employed in theoretical science, he did not distinguish what I regard as the primary sense of the word, namely the production of change by the deliberate activity of a human agent; but several of his incidental remarks seem to me to require the recognition of this sense as prior to all the three which he discusses. In his account of the concept of cause in theoretical science, i.e. of causal laws, Collingwood rejected the regularity view put forward by empiricists, which is the one I have adopted; I think that his criticism, particularly of Russell's theory, rests on the mistaken assumption that inductive inference must be justified by deductive. The general distinction which I have drawn between efficient causation as deliberate activity and causal laws as universal regularity of sequence, together with the view that animism is responsible for thinking of the second as 'causal', is to be found in Reid's *Essays on the Active Powers of Man.*

'Efficient cause', then, means the activity that makes a change. 'Causal law' means a statement of regular sequence of change. The first has nothing to do with 'law' (regularity in a *class* of changes) or with 'necessity' (*universality* of regular sequence), and the second has nothing to do with making. An efficient cause, in the context where we acquire the original idea of it, i.e. in our own activity, is of its nature voluntary, not forced. It is contrasted with being *passively* affected, with changes of mental state which we do not initiate. Where the change is one initiated by us, we can act or not act, as we choose. If the situation is not of that nature, then it is not a case of *acting,* of our causing the change. To say that we 'are forced to do' something means that we are passive, not active; the change takes place without chosen activity on our part, and contrary to the way in which we would choose to act. So we think of it as due to the activity of some other person (where we are compelled by other men, or believe that we are compelled by God), or of some 'force' (where, in the absence of a person, we apply the faded animistic analogy to things). When we say that a man is 'forced' by threats or weapons to do what he would otherwise not choose to do, he is of course not passive; it is he that effects the change demanded. But then, strictly, he has the choice of acting, or refusing to act and suffering whatever is threatened. He is 'forced' to act in the sense that very few human beings *would* choose the unpleasant alternative. When the act (e.g., the divulging of secret information) is wrung from him by torture such as to make him 'lose control of himself', he is strictly forced, for he does not then choose to speak; the event (the speech) takes place passively, not from his active choice—somewhat, but not quite (because the tortured man is aware of what is going on), like what happens when a man talks in his sleep. It is a situation of which it would not be sophistical to say (adapting the notorious line of Euripides),

ἡ γλῶσσ' ἐφώνησ' ἡ δὲ φρὴν ἀναίτιος.

When, however, a person is responsible as having actively (deliberately) caused a change, he was free to act or refrain. The idea of freedom to choose is implied in the very conception of a cause (activity) as we attribute it to ourselves. When a person does choose, he has regard to motives, to purposes (as was said before, he acts *for* a purpose), but it is he, not they, that is the efficient cause.

If now a psychological law is discovered, that actions are always (or in a certain percentage of instances) preceded by the manifestation of a particular type of motive, e.g. desire for personal advantage, this is a 'causal' law. It does not say that the desire is the efficient cause. As a scientific statement it has nothing to do with efficient causes. If, as was suggested earlier, the name of 'causal law' is restricted to 100% regularities of sequence, then a psychological statement of regularity is to be called a causal law only if it asserts a universal connexion. The statement that human actions are *always* preceded by self-interested desire, if confirmed by all observed instances, would be a 'causal law'. The statement that the vast majority of human actions are preceded by such desire, if confirmed by instances, would report a regularity of less than 100%, and so would not be called a 'causal law' according to the definition of that expression which we have suggested, but would be, and in fact is, none the less a useful law for psychology and social science generally. Few pyschological laws of behaviour are in fact causal laws, i.e. statements of necessary (universally regular) sequence. The 'forced' action of a man at the pistol's point is not necessary (i.e., an example of a universal regularity), but it is highly probable. Most men would do the act demanded, but a few would refuse and choose to be killed instead. Hence such action is not strictly 'forced' in the sense of necessarily (universally) taking place. Accordingly, the general statement, that men threatened at the pistol's point do as they are told, is not a 'causal law', but can still be used as a scientific law, asserting a regularity of less than 100%. The general statement, treated by some psychologists as a law, that aggressive behaviour 'results from' (i.e., is regularly preceded by) frustration, likewise asserts a regularity of high frequency but not a universal sequence.

Causal laws are one type of scientific laws, general statements asserting regularities. Efficient causation is free activity. The problem of free will *versus* determinism has arisen from ambiguity of the word 'cause', as the result of the rise of natural science *before* our primitive conception of material change had been purged of its animism. Hence the 'laws' of nature were called 'causal'. In fact, the language of science deals with events as falling under regular classes, while the language used in everyday life about human action describes certain events as caused (i.e., actively or deliberately initiated) by persons for the sake of purposes. The two languages are quite different, expressing two different points of view, and there is no conflict between them. You might as well say there is a conflict between regarding a chess set as thirty-two pieces of wood and regarding it as the parts of a game. Both judgements are true, and there is no conflict between them. Deliberate actions are looked at, from the point of view of an agent, as being the (free) causing of changes by a person; they do not need to be chosen. They are also observed, from the point of view of an uninvolved spectator, to follow certain sequences. Both points of view report legitimate interpretations of experience, and both therefore may be called true, just as the two statements about the chess set are true.

It may be noted that Hume's view of the problem of free will is, in essentials, the one set out here, and is in line with his explanation of the necessity attributed to causal laws. The best statement of his view is in Section VII of the *Enquiry concerning Human Understanding*. His discussion in the text, however, is not an admission of libertarianism, as he claims it is. For the freedom that he there accepts is freedom as opposed to external constraint, i.e., *social* freedom; the *moral* freedom of libertarianism is neglected in the text, and Hume, after allowing freedom as opposed to constraint, merely says that freedom as opposed to necessity is the same as chance. But in a note,[1] Hume turns to moral freedom and gives an account of that, which is in line with his epistemological discussion of necessity, and which seems to have received little attention from his commentators. Hume says he holds that both determinism and libertarianism are true. For a spectator, or for the agent reflecting on his act when done, an act is compared with similar acts performed in similar circumstances in the past, and its resemblance to these induces, in the person so reflecting, the usual feeling of compulsion, so that he attributes necessity to the act. But the agent, at the time of acting, does not reflect on the resemblance of the circumstances and of the proposed action to past circumstances and acts; consequently, for him the feeling of compulsion, which would be aroused by such comparative reflection, does not occur, and the absence of this feeling of compulsion (or, as Hume calls the absence, a fictitious feeling of 'looseness') is the psychological ground of the agent's thought that he is not necessitated, that he is free either to act or not to act. Thus the act is both necessary (for a spectator, or for the agent on subsequent reflection) and free (for the agent at the unreflective moment of action). That is, in the one case there is felt a compulsion to think of the action being performed, in the other there is not.

In referring earlier to Hume's account of the 'necessity' of

[1]On p. 94 of Selby-Bigge's edition.

causal laws, I accepted his view that this necessity could justifiably be interpreted only as universality, and I rejected his psychological account of how we come to attribute necessity in the sense of compulsion; I suggested that there he confuses the compulsion of passivity, which is opposed to the freedom of activity, both referring to a particular occasion, with the necessity of causal laws, which refers to the regularity of sequence among a class of pairs of events. In his discussion of free will, his description of the psychological grounds for the two points of view is again unacceptable, and here again this is because he confuses the 'necessity' of causal laws with the felt compulsion of being passively affected by a supposed efficient cause. According to Hume's account, if I think, when struck by a falling sack of potatoes, that the sack is 'making' me fall, I must be reflecting, while being struck, that in the past when I (or other people) have been struck by sacks of potatoes or similar weighty objects, I (or they) have fallen. This is not so absurd as it sounds at first hearing, if for 'reflecting' we substitute some far less self-conscious state of thought; even then, however, it would only explain why I think there 'must' be a fall (in fact, I should think there would probably, not certainly, be a fall), and would not explain why I say the sack of potatoes is 'making' or 'causing' me to fall. His account also implies that if I say, when I am tired, that I am not compelled to sit down, I am less reflective than when I was being struck by the sack of potatoes. Apart from the psychology, however, Hume's doctrine of the two points of view, from one of which a man is determined, from the other free, is very helpful, and it is from considering this section of Hume that I have reached my own account. From the outlook of scientific observation (Hume's spectator), a man's act is 'explained' by bringing it under a regular law through comparison with similar acts in similar circumstances; it is dealt with as a 'thing' or event observed, and as liable to be correlated with similar observed events ('things happening'). From the outlook of agents (which may be taken not only by the actual agent, as Hume suggests, but also by spectators thinking of themselves as potential agents, imagining themselves in the actual agent's shoes, instead of thinking of the situation detachedly as an external object of their observation), the act is considered, not in relation to similar past acts, but as issuing from a freely choosing and responsible 'person'. The distinction between the approach of a detached, scientific observer and that of an agent, is a distinction between interpreting what we find as 'things happening' and as 'persons acting', between thinking of 'events' and thinking of 'actions'.

§3. *The laws of human behaviour*

In my suggested solution of the problem of free will, there is one point that may be overlooked, giving rise to an objection. Let us put the objection first, so as to bring out the point clearly. It may be urged that the suggested resolution of inconsistency between ethics and science is merely superficial, leaving the real inconsistency beneath the surface. There may be no inconsistency in saying that deliberate acts are both freely caused and fall under regular sequences, but is there not an inconsistency in what is implied here? If the agent could have acted otherwise, then, had he done so, his act would not have fallen under the law under which it in fact falls. Surely the admission that acts fall under laws implies that they could not have been different from what they are.

This objection would be valid only if the laws of human action were laws of 100% regularity. If, for example, desire for one's own advantage were *always* followed by action directed at that, then it *would* be pointless to say that an agent, having such a desire, could act against his own interest. But in fact the statistical laws of human behaviour are not laws of 100% regularity. Nor, I think, are the laws of animal behaviour always such. Empirical psychology and the other social sciences would be in a poor pass if they restricted themselves to universal laws. It should be noted that I speak of the laws of *behaviour*, psychological laws. *Physiological* laws are usually (or perhaps always) laws of 100% regularity. The establishment of the science of physiology with its universal causal laws, however, did nothing to move back the frontiers of free will in the libertarian conceptions of the plain man. The plain man who insists that by efforts of will he could have risen a little earlier or could make himself a little fitter, knows perfectly well that he cannot do without sleep altogether or turn himself into an Olympic record-breaker; and he knew this before physiology became an established science. His own experience suggests to him what is later exhibited in the nature of the scientific laws concerned, namely, that effort of will can do little or nothing in the face of physiological conditions but can do something in the face of psychological conditions. Universal laws can be found in the physical sciences, at least at the macroscopic level. (Whether or not they can at the sub-microscopic level is not to my purpose; I do not found any arguments about human behaviour on the discussion of the uncertainty principle in atomic physics, though the fact remains that that subject *can* proceed with laws asserting probability of less than 100%.) Universal laws cannot, however, be found (or at least, not often) in the social sciences, and not always in the biological. It is sometimes represented that the social sciences are thereby defective, that their laws would be universal if only we know enough, and that these studies must not adopt the title of 'sciences' until the day of revelation when their laws can truly ape the laws of physics. Such dogmatism does little service to the social sciences, and is far from the empirical attitude on which science has flourished. To the sciences above all should be applied the old saying, 'By their fruits shall ye know them', and the social sciences have made considerable progress since the day when Hobbes, in deliberately applying the procedure of natural science to the study of man and society, thought he could treat it as a branch of physics. Psychological hedonism enunciated a universal law for human behaviour, explicitly carrying over an analogy from mechanics, and psychological hedonism is absurd more for the analogy than for its final assertions. The tale of Buridan's ass is greeted by an untutored audience with guffaws, simply because it is ludicrous to think of an animal behaving as iron filings behave in the presence of magnets. On the contrary, we talk of iron filings 'being attracted' to a magnet, through analogy with our being attracted by an object of desire. Then to reverse the analogy, with the stiff trappings of mechanical universal laws, is absurd. (I know that the word 'attraction', as applied to a mental state, is in turn a metaphor from the external world, where men draw ropes and horses draw carts. Most of the language we use to describe what goes on in the mind, is derived in this way by metaphor from the language used to describe what we observe in the external world, for talk about the latter came first. But talk about human feelings and desires came before scientific talk about magnets and iron filings. The unreflective development of language contains analogies of second and third order, just as reflective metaphysics does.) The laws of the regular sequences of human behaviour have a probability of less than 100%, but they are not thereby rendered useless. If people often (or usually) act from self-interest, it is possible to schematize their economic behaviour taking that motive alone into account, as classical economics does, and if we do so we shall not go far wrong. Insurance companies get on well enough by banking on a rough repetition of frequencies, but they do not become insolvent if there is a slight change, as there often is; they work within rough limits and allow for such changes. If we bank on hearing the truth from a man known to be usually honest, we shall not go far wrong; but this does not imply that we shall *never* find him telling a lie.

It should be noted that I am not resting the defence of free will on the *present* state of empirical psychology and the other social sciences, and envisaging the possibility that the case might be lost in the future if the social sciences were so improved as to set out universal laws. If that did happen (and it is not logically impossible), I should indeed cease to maintain a case for free will, for I do not see how it can truthfully be said that a man could have acted otherwise than he did, if his act falls under a universal regularity; the regularity would not be universal if an alternative act, alleged to be possible, had taken place. But the supposition that the laws of human behaviour could be universal laws, though not logically impossible, is, as things are, factually impossible. Consider any such law that might be suggested, e.g., that men buy in the cheapest available market and sell in the dearest. This general statement can be used as a perfectly good law of economics. It is not universal, but an economist might perfectly well be able, for his particular purpose, to ignore the exceptions. If, however, a would-be mechanizer of economics asserted that the statement expresses a universal or 'inexorable' law, as inexorable as the laws of mechanics, anyone could easily refute his theory merely by deciding, purely for the sake of such refutation, to go out into the street, look at the prices of apples in several shops, and buy a pound at the dearest price, or by advertising some article for sale and then deliberately, for the sake of refuting the dogmatist, offering the article to the lowest bidder. Economists can safely ignore such quixotic, and perhaps other, exceptions to their generalization, but they cannot turn the generalization into an inexorable, universal law. Plain facts of common-sense knowledge, not the present state of the social sciences, are sufficient to show that the laws of human behaviour are not universal. They are the same plain facts that lead men to say that they have a measure of free will, and these facts cannot be contradicted by any advance of the social sciences to greater precision, which will of course take place. They could be contradicted by some miraculous (or, I supose, evolutionary) change in the nature of human beings, but that would be a change in the facts studied by the social sciences, and not a change in the nature or methods of the sciences. No doubt the free activity of scientific inquiry would become impossible if such a change in human nature did take place, but a scientific God or Martian could still frame the (then universal) laws governing the behaviour of terrestrial human beings. As things are, it is not an imperfection in the social sciences that renders their laws less than universal, and they are not to be denied the name of sciences because of the non-universal character of their laws.

§4. *Regularity and rational action*

Nevertheless, it will be said, must we not account for the fact that there are highly regular, though not universal, laws of human behaviour? Must there not be some reason why deliberate human actions, though freely chosen, follow fairly regular patterns and are not relatively random? Certainly there must, and the reason is that human beings, when acting deliberately, are fairly *consistent* beings. They set up rules or principles of action for themselves, or accept such rules from others, and for the most part they stick to these rules. This is part of what we mean (or imply) by saying they are rational. It is also the reason why the language of morals can and does assume a high degree of consistency. That assumption is not, as has sometimes been urged, an objection to free will, though it is an argument against a theory that human actions take place by chance or at random, and accordingly it is an argument in favour of the weak form of 'determinism' (if that name, though strictly inappropriate, be insisted upon) which I allow, namely the view that human behaviour can be brought under scientific 'laws' of regularity. To act rationally means, in one sense and in part, to follow rules or principles of action consistently. This is only part of the meaning of 'rational' as applied to conduct, for 'rational' principles of action must be based on 'rational' beliefs, where 'rational' means in accordance with the lessons of experience. A man who believes that motor-cars cannot harm him, and who accordingly adopts a principle of crossing roads whatever the state of traffic, would hardly be called rational; and a man who consistently thinks he is Napoleon, and acts as if he were, is a lunatic despite his consistency. Wisdom involves not merely living according to principles, as opposed to haphazard obedience to whims of the moment, but also framing and modifying those principles in the light of experience.

Consistency (or 'rationality') of action, such as I have described, is of course not confined to acting in accordance with *moral* principles. There can equally be a consistent egoism, and there could (logically at least) be consistent malice. 'Evil be thou my Good' expresses a resolution to do wrong actions on principle, a deliberate adoption of consistent vice. Consistent malice may be psychologically impossible in human action (though Iago is perhaps intended to be an imaginary example of it), but there can certainly be consistent egoism. Indeed, the rules of prudence furnish a more obvious example than moral rules of the statement that a 'rational' man is one who adopts and consistently follows rules or principles of action, and this is why the 'economic man' of classical economics was assumed to be an egoistic hedonist. Moralists who speak as if moral action alone could be rational, introduce confusion. I may deliberately follow a consistent policy of treating all persons as ends, and then we have the rationality of moral action. But I may no less deliberately and consistently follow a policy of treating myself alone as an end, and then we have a rational egoism. (Hence moralists like Butler and Sidgwick fallaciously think of 'cool' or 'rational' egoism, i.e., of action according to the *principle* of seeking one's happiness on the whole, as being 'rational' also in the sense of morally obligatory.) Of course, the adoption by everyone of consistent egoism would lead to 'inconsistency' with each other in practice, in that their policies would often clash and so be, when universally adopted, impracticable; whereas the universal adoption of the policy of treating all persons as ends would not involve this type of clash, and so might be called 'universally consistent' in a sense in which egoism is not. This, perhaps, is one way in which Kant's first formulation of the Categorical Imperative is linked with his second formulation. But 'consistency' is then used in a different sense from that in which egoism may be a consistent policy.

Likewise it is, I think, a mistake to confine the occurrence of free will (i.e., of exercising, or failing to exercise when we could, deliberate and effective effort) to situations of moral 'temptation', where pressing desires conflict with thought of duty. (This restriction of the scope of free will is made, e.g., by Dr. Carritt in *The Theory of Morals* and *Ethical and Political Thinking,* and by Professor C. A. Campbell in his Inaugural Address, *In Defence of Free Will.)* We can just as much exercise, or fail to exercise, the effort required to follow a principle or rational policy of egoism against the pressure of immediate inclinations, and these inclinations may be benevolent no less than (immediately and, in the light of the principle, illusively) selfish. Suppose I had formed a habit of acting from benevolent impulse whenever that occurred; I could then resolve to follow in future a deliberate policy of egoism, and the carrying out of this resolution would involve efforts of will when my (at present) habitual benevolence prompted me to act against my interest. The policy, and often the individual exercise of the effort to follow it against benevolence, would be wrong, but the pursuit of the policy would be 'rational', i.e. consistent, and the exercise of effort would be free. It may be replied, on behalf of the restrictionists, that the only sound argument for free will lies in the implications of moral obligation. But that argument, that 'ought' implies 'can', applies no less to the non-moral 'ought'; for so-called 'hypothetical imperatives' include a requirement upon the agent as well as a hypothetical statement depending on a causal law. 'You ought to try arsenic', when suggested to a would-be murderer, not only states that if arsenic is administered it will do the desired trick, but also states a requirement upon the murderer if his practice is to be consistent with his professed purpose. The requirement is not a moral one, but a quasi-logical requirement of consistency between action and adopted purpose,[1] and it is made only where the act required is thought to be within the agent's power.

It is not difficult to explain why deliberate human actions, moral or non-moral, are fairly regular. The difficulty is to explain why material events are apparently completely regular. If we are dissatisfied with our ignorance about regularity in

[1]Cf. ch. iv, §2, and ch. viii, §3, above.

material change, and insist on suggesting a reason for it, then, I submit, the only suggestion we can make is to draw an analogy from the sphere of deliberate human action, where we see how regularity comes about. This procedure is natural enough for *some* events that are not deliberate acts. For we find in ourselves, that after we have for a time consistently willed acts of a certain kind, they then become habitual and occur without deliberate volition but retaining the character in other respects of the original willed acts. Hence, in discussing the 'instinctive' behaviour of animals, we say they act *as if* they (or someone on their behalf) had deliberated a means to a foreseen end. We interpret their behaviour teleologically, i.e., on the analogy of deliberate human activity, or of habitual human behaviour that has come to be what it is as the result of consistent deliberate activity. Applying the analogy to the inanimate world, the regularity of material events then suggests that they are due to rational decision, the result of rational activity. This suggestion gives a possible argument for the existence of a God. Virtually it is Berkeley's argument, but unlike Berkeley's it is not a *demonstration,* for I do not think that an agnostic phenomenalism, which refuses to ask *why* events happen as they do, involves any self-contradiction, nor have we proved that there could not be a consistent efficient cause different in kind from the activity of persons. The argument is merely an analogical suggestion, to be used only if we are dissatisfied with our ignorance as to why material events should be universally regular. No doubt many people would wish to give the argument stronger force than that. They would urge that we cannot possibly rest content with ignorance; we must say that all events have *some* cause, i.e. efficient cause, and if the only efficient causes we know are persons we are bound to infer such a cause for material events. This is an appeal to the causal axiom ('Every change happens through being produced by an efficient cause'), and I doubt if the causal axiom is known to be universally true; at any rate, there is no self-contradiction in denying it. We acquire our idea of an efficient cause from our own activity, in which we produce change, and we are thereby inclined to think of all changes as being of this sort, namely, produced by an efficient cause. But might not this, too, be merely a relic of projective animism? We find changes caused by ourselves, and we find other changes among the objects of our passive experience. I do not see any necessity for fusing the two types into one. But we can reasonably ask why material events fall under universally regular laws, the chances for which, among all the alternative possibilities of the relations of events to each other, would seem to be minute; and it is then at least a justifiable suggestion to say, by analogy, that the regularity may be the result of rational activity.

It should, however, be noted that our problematic argument for the existence of a God does not, taken by itself, imply the God of theism, for it implies neither omnipotence nor goodness. It suggests more the *Νοῦς* of Anaxagoras and of Plato's *Timaeus,* reason imposing order on chaos and in the face of ἀνάγκη (which we usually translate 'necessity' but is better rendered, in this context, 'brute obstruction'). In fact, this Greek conception obviously likens the cosmic process to the human struggle to order one's life in the face of an obstructive (but using that word without suggestion of *purposeful* obstruction) nature. Since speculative metaphysics must be analogical from human experience if it is to convey any meaning, such a view is intelligible and deserving of attention if we are to have metaphysical hypotheses at all.

I suggest, then, that the laws of science do nothing to undermine the existence of voluntary causation in deliberate human action. If we are to seek any interrelation between these two things, we must, conversely, say that the character of human action suggests that the regularity of nature is due to rational activity. But if we eschew speculative metaphysics, and stick to the interpretations of experience conveyed in established language of the plain man or of a long and successfully practised specialism, then we simply have two ways of looking at human behaviour, with no conflict between them.

My account, of course, does not fully elucidate the nature

of voluntary activity, and I do not pretend that such elucidation is an easy task or one that should be neglected. But this is not the place for me to attempt it, even if I felt competent to do so. I have been concerned in this book with moral judgement, not with moral (or non-moral) choice. Moral judgements presuppose the existence of free choice, and the objection of determinism, raised from a particular interpretation of scientific procedure, claims to dispose of the existence of free choice and so to put out of court any description of its nature. It is enough for my present purpose to show that that interpretation of scientific procedure is false, and that the presuppositions of moral judgement do not conflict with those of scientific procedure.

One further remark should be added, however, in case some of my statements be taken to suggest that I regard the scope of free will as unlimited or at least very wide. I do not think this. My conception of the scope of free will is derived from what I take to be well-established interpretation of experience, while the objection to it that I have discussed is an objection arising from the confused theory of determinism. To remove the trammels of false theory does not absolve us from then attending to the limitations found in the normal interpretation of experience, and to the modifications of that interpretation induced by the revealing, in the course of scientific investigation, of observable, but hitherto unnoticed or insufficiently noticed, facts. The exercise of effective deliberate activity seems to me to be confined within comparatively narrow limits (though not restricted to moral and immoral action). The position of the narrow boundaries shifts as character changes, but some of the changes in character are the result of frequent and consistent exercise of effort, and therefore, although the difference that effort can make at any particular time is small, over a long period the cumulative effect of repeated and consistent effort in one direction may be considerable. Thus I am not much inclined to attribute fully moral responsibility to particular acts of great consequence; I do not believe, for example, that many murders could have been prevented by mere effort of will by the agent at the particular moment of commission. But this does not mean that the effect of moral exertion, or of exertion in the direction of non-moral principles of action, is, in human life as a whole, negligible. On the contrary, I think that such exertion ('practical reason'), combined with intellectual exertion ('theoretical reason'), can make and has made a great difference to the course of human history.

INDEX

For Product Safety Concerns and Information please contact our EU representative GPSR@taylorandfrancis.com Taylor & Francis Verlag GmbH, Kaufingerstraße 24, 80331 München, Germany

Batch number: 10725802

Printed by Printforce, the Netherlands